Rests
and Repetition
in Music

The Robinswood Press
Stourbridge   England

Rests and Repetition in Music

by

Christoph Peter

Translated from the original German edition by Alan Stott

Zum Phänomen der Pause und der Wiederholung in der Musik

Bund der Freien Waldorfschulen Stuttgart 1986

© Christoph Peter

This Translation © Alan Stott 1992

The Robinswood Press
Stourbridge   England

ISBN 1 869981 45 6

Original German Essay titles:

Die Pause in der Musik und ihre Analogie im Leben und in der Erziehung

THE REST IN MUSIC
Its Analogy in Life and Education

and

Die Wiederholung in der Musik, ihre Bedeutung und ihre Anwendung in der Erziehung und im Musikunterricht

REPETITION IN MUSIC
Its Significance and Use in Education and the Teaching of Music

The support of the Pädagogische Forschungsstelle beim Bund der Freien Waldorfschulen, Stuttgart, for this English edition is appreciated.

All Rights reserved. No part of this publication may be reproduced, stored in a retrieval system, or transmitted, in any form, or by any means, electronic, mechanical, photocopying, recording or otherwise, without the prior permission in writing, from the publisher.

Typeset by Wynstones Press Gloucester
Printed and bound in Great Britain by Billings and Sons Ltd Worcester

CONTENTS

		Page
	PREFACE (to the Original German Edition)	1
	INTRODUCTION - Christoph Peter	2

I THE REST IN MUSIC

1	Introduction	5
2	Basic Points in Considering Rests	7
3	Examples from Musical Works	
	a) From the Baroque Period	11
	b) From the Classical Period	20
	c) From the Romantic Period	33
4	Index of Examples	40

II THE REST IN LIFE AND EDUCATION

1	Nature and the Human Being	42
2	Enthusiasm and Discipline	43
3	The Breath Rest as Expression of Inner Calm	44
4	The Variety of Phenomena	45
5	Readiness: the Basis of Mutual Understanding and the Source of Inner Calm	48

III REPETITION IN MUSIC

1	Introduction	50
2	Repetition in Music and its Significance	
	a) Antiquity	51
	b) The Middle Ages	52
	c) The Renaissance	54
	d) The Baroque Era	57
	e) Classicism	66
	f) Romanticism	79
	g) Modern Times	84

IV   THE USE OF REPETITION IN TEACHING AND EDUCATION

1	Introduction	88
2	Imitation	90
3	Breath and Consciousness	91
4	Development	95
5	Transformation	97
6	The Calmness and Strength of Rhythmical Repetition in Life and in Education.	98

BIBLIOGRAPHY   100

GLOSSARY

ENGLISH	AMERICAN
Minim	Half-note
Crotchet	Quarter-note
Quaver	Eighth-note
Semiquaver	Sixteenth-note
Bar	Measure
Bar line	Bar
Note	Tone
Part-writing	Voice-leading
Pedal-point	Organ-point
Class	Grade
Primary School	Elementary School

PREFACE TO THE ORIGINAL GERMAN EDITION

The first of these two essays by Christoph Peter was written at the end of his college studies in 1952, the second at the end of his teacher training in 1955. They were not meant for publication. However, with the increase of his lecturing activities during the last fifteen years of his life, and above all after the posthumous appearance of his book *'Die Sprache der Musik in Mozarts "Zauberflöte"'* (published by Verlag Freies Geistesleben. Stuttgart. 1983; English manuscript translation: 'The language of music in Mozart's "Magic Flute"'), the idea of making these early works more widely available grew more and more persistent.

In publishing these studies we should like to emphasize that Christoph Peter, were he alive today, would no doubt have revised them to some extent, altering certain formulations, probably deleting some points specifically linked to circumstances at the time of writing, and expanding several topics. It would not do to tamper with his text; it seemed best to let these studies appear as they stand.

Christoph Peter found he had a close affinity with the ideas of Rudolf Steiner from an early stage, especially with the remarks on 'the inaudible in music'. During his student days, Peter was already active as a pianist for eurythmy. This work confirmed his conviction — which clearly emerges in these essays — that the rightness and fruitfulness of these ideas could be directly demonstrable in music itself and that the novel approach to thinking and feeling Steiner had introduced could be fully integrated into musical education and practice. This conviction, which confirms the life-enhancing qualities of these stimuli, he tried untiringly to make a concrete reality in his work.

That these two works, with their choice of theme and methods of treatment, are impressive as pioneering achievements even today, thirty years after their inception, is a remarkable testimony to the spiritual independence and creative strength of the author.

It is in this sense that we may wish for the widest possible circulation of these 'seeds'.

Stuttgart/Dornach Veronika Peter
June 1986 Felix Lindenmaier

INTRODUCTION

Christoph Peter was born on 11 October 1927 in Munich, and died on 3 August 1982 in Zürich.

With Christoph Peter's death, the musical world and the Waldorf School movement lost one of the vital, towering personalities stamped with a living musicality.

As a child, Christoph grew up in a musical environment, for his father worked as a violinist in the Staatstheater (City Theatre), Munich. He showed his competence already in his early years in a practical way as a pianist for eurythmy. After training as a school musician at the Musikhochschule (Academy of Music), Munich, from 1948 to 1952, and graduating in 1953 from the Lehrerseminar (Teachers' Seminary), Stuttgart, he concluded his training from 1953 to 1955 with two significant essays which were published together in book form in 1986, of which the present volume is the English translation. Further studies in composition with Fritz Büchtger, chamber music with Enrico Mainardi in Salzburg, and piano with Hans Leygraf in Hannover allowed him to develop his musical talents. He also received the greatest encouragement during his training from Hans Mersmann, Maria Landes-Hindemith, Richard Jacobj, Anny von Lange, Otte E. Crusius and others. From 1955-1977 he worked as music teacher at the Freien Waldorfschule (Free Waldorf School), Hannover; from 1967 he was a visiting lecturer and from 1977 until his death in 1982, resident music tutor at the Teachers' Seminary for Waldorf Education, Stuttgart.

The Foreword to the work which has become his legacy, *'Die Sprache der Musik in Mozarts "Zauberflöte"'* ('The language of music in Mozart's "Magic Flute"'), rightly acknowledges the stimulus Peter received for his own research from the creative suggestions of Rudolf Steiner. Steiner's indication that the 'unheard in music', the actual musical element, lies 'between the notes', was of special significance for Christoph Peter. Thus it was important for him to work repeatedly on the quality of the inaudible. This was stamped on his style as *conductor* and *player*. While paying attention to the inaudible element between the notes, listening can be trained differently from the first steps onwards. Only from now on do notes become 'windows into the spiritual'. In eurythmy the unheard becomes visible, because the essential thing lies in showing the process of *coming into being*, not in fixed positions. Herein lies the beginning of Peter's research into the different qualities and effects of the *rest in music*. All this insight won in music became a decisive influence for Peter's entire life's work, essentially influencing his pedagogy and his compositions and, not least, lending life to his piano playing.

It was true of him as *music teacher*, drawing completely from artistic involvement: if music was to be a protection against the destructive forces of our time, then the basis of this must be laid in the correct musical education of the child. It may be said that Peter's educational influence was and still is widely recognized. It seemed to him so important to activate a child, already at an early age, against the influence of the technical world of the media, through stimulating live music-making and in practising education of the will, and in promoting and strengthening the finding of personality. The collaboration of instrumental teachers and school musicians was of great importance for him. Thus he also prepared the basis for founding the Freie Musikschule (Free Music School) in Hannover, which enjoys a close contact with the Waldorf School.

Despite his strenuous involvement in education, Christoph Peter leaves behind a rich output of compositions, covering most areas. Chamber music (a string quartet, five piano trios), works for soloist and orchestra, pieces for piano and strings, sonatas for violin and organ, sonatas for solo instruments, an opera based on *Die Versunkene Glocke* (The Submerged Bell) of Gerhard Hauptmann, and music for plays: above all, highly significant music for the four Mystery Dramas of Rudolf Steiner (the music for the third and fourth play completed after his death by Peter-Michael Riehm). Of his thirteen Cantatas, a *Cantata for Michaelmas* should be mentioned, the *Hymn of Notker Balbulus*, an *Easter Cantata* and a *Whitsun Cantata*, a *Cantata* in three parts to poems by Albert Steffen, and the *Assisi Cantata* in two parts. Furthermore, he wrote a quantity of music for The Act of Consecration of Man (and other sacraments of The Christian Community) for different combinations of instruments: songs, song-cantatas and other works. A rich harvest for so short an earthly life! It is important here to remember that his compositions always came into existence as a result of requests for quite special occasions. His maxim was to serve a need, to stand back quietly and modestly, to be of service. Peter's compositions have been performed in Germany, Switzerland, England, Sweden, USA and Canada.

Apart from the two studies mentioned above, Christoph Peter left behind his basic, important and extensive book on Mozart's *Magic Flute*, the outcome of thirty years intensive research into every possible musically relevant aspect. This book can be regarded as a pioneer work of Mozart research. A more profound work on Mozart's masterpiece could hardly be found.

As a *lecturer*, Peter contributed to countless conferences. From the wealth of lecture themes the following could be mentioned: 'Time and the Timeless', 'Man and Music between Polarities', 'Polar Streams in Music', 'What is the Relationship of Rudolf Steiner's Suggestions for Music and Music of the Twentieth Century?', 'Ways to a New Musical Listening', 'The Inaudible in Music', 'Ways to an Experience of the Octave', 'Concord and Discord Today', etc., apart from many different educational themes.

As a musician, it was clear to him that whoever *teaches* music should also be a practising musician. For this reason he repeatedly undertook extended concert tours as pianist of the Peter Trio, for whom he wrote his piano trios. We learnt to appreciate him as an excellent performer.

Together with his wife Veronika Peter, who was an active performer of his compositions and involved with his musical work, he initiated conferences and sought to achieve a closer contact between eurythmy and music. Conferences of professional musicians for mutual exchange and for stimulation lay close to his heart. He was also involved in the collaboration of priests and musicians. He initiated courses for young people which offered not only opportunities to hear about and meet anthroposophy, but to include it as a vital part of personal practice and work (Chamber Music Conferences at Engelberg). Music weekends devoted to special problems in listening to new music came into existence in Stuttgart under the theme, 'Change in Listening to Music'.

In concluding these observations on an earthly existence all too soon ended, let us remember the special qualities which imbued his being: his profoundly human loving-kindness, his modesty and warmth of heart which were received with deep gratitude by all who knew him; lastly, the ever rarer art of taking time to listen, which made him outstanding in so many areas of life.

Herman Pfrogner

I THE REST IN MUSIC

Its Analogy in Life and Education

1) Introduction

Rests arise out of some inner necessity, from some force that is effective in bringing the flow in a certain event to a halt. The event can be all-embracing but can also relate to the most inconspicuous processes of development in nature or in man. Two factors are decisive for the intrinsic value of a rest: the point in the inner dynamic of the passage in which it occurs, and its length. On the basis of both these factors we come to three basic types of rests.

The first type embraces all rests which commence shortly before the climax or the lowest point of the dynamic curve and outlast it. We will call them *transformation rests*. The following shows this diagrammatically:

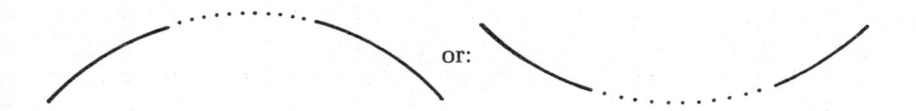

The second type arises when a rest starts at a dynamic rise or fall, and does not outlast the turning point. We will call them *rests of direction*.

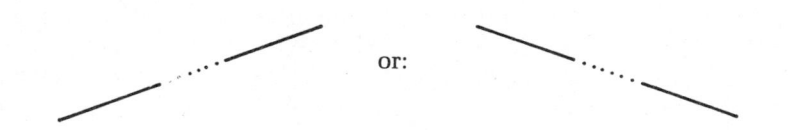

The third type is the rest which begins and ends in a dynamically quiet part of a passage. This is none other than the first type of rest in a diminished form, or reversed, within an especially large curve, during the length of its low point. We will call them *rests of potentiality*. They can be diagrammatically shown in the following ways:

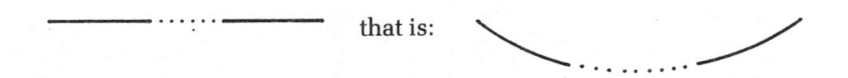

While in the first two types something quite definite occurs (with the first, the transformation and, with the second, the continuation of the general direction) here nothing seems to happen. This is, however, a contradiction, for each rest is part of a whole. It is, therefore, as I have tried to express with the term (rest of potentiality), filled with a certain feeling of expectancy, which can in fact imply considerable tension.

With the naming of rests and the indication of their inner value we have already implied that the rest need not mean a complete 'nothingness'. To someone who is completely insensitive to the inner dynamic of an event, it may well appear as though nothing has occurred. This does not detract from the facts as described above. It only makes clear that the intrinsic sense for such an event is not necessarily given. It has to be developed. This is possible to a special degree with the experience of rests. While normally the outer event fits with the inner, often all too easily hiding it, the remaining flow is brought to a standstill in the rest, allowing the inner dynamic and movement to appear for a short time more clearly. We become aware of this inner dynamic and mobility. And if we become engrossed in a rest in which this inner stream also comes to rest as in the rest of potentiality, or for moments in the corresponding transition rests, then we experience the significance and importance of an unnamed, creative force which is effective precisely in this rest.

2) Basic Points in Considering Rests

The occurrence of rests in music is incredibly manifold. It is impossible to describe them exactly and award each one its due, especially as the three basic types mentioned above often appear combined. For example, a rest can be seen as a rest of direction taken as a whole, but on the other hand it can be viewed separately as a transition rest. We shall therefore only describe the most essential points in the examples below (pp 12-39). For rests in music, besides the three basic factors mentioned, the following come into consideration: the three basic elements of music (rhythm, melody and harmony); furthermore, dynamics, form and part-writing (not in the sense of polyphony, but taken as a whole).

From the point of view of rhythm (1), the following rests can be listed:

a) Rest on the downbeat

Pulse relies on its main downbeat (especially 4/4 time). When a rest falls on a downbeat, the following movement acquires a certain winged quality or even a strong forward impulse

b) Rest on the beat (excluding the downbeat rest)

This does not have that deep effect. It often appears after final chords

c) Shortening rest

This lightens up , similar to the inconspicuous but not unimportant:

d) Non-legato rest

This is not indicated by a rest symbol but is implied through phrase-marks (♩♩♩ or ♩♩♩ or ♩♩♩ etc.). It also occurs in pizzicato passages of string instruments. Especially with constant repetition in a continuous movement, it points to the usual qualities of rests.

e) Rests depending on their connection to the previous rhythmical note-values

We shall illustrate this with a particularly interesting example. It should be mentioned in general that a rest after quick movement appears longer than one after slow movement.

f) Held-on notes

In a correspondingly quick movement, these can give the effect of rests (𝄽 ♩ | ♩)

In melody the following rests occur:

a) Phrasing rest

This appears after small phrases, for example, after feminine endings. After larger phrases it is covered by the breathing rest.

b) Breathing rest

This is the 'most natural' rest in music. It is not only significant in vocal music. When rightly observed by performers, it affects the natural breathing rhythm of the listener in instrumental music, too.

c) The interruption of a melodic phrase

This is usually the transition stage of the uninterrupted movement to a rest, or vice versa.

d) The inner 'built-in' rest

Within a melody, this forms part of the melodic flow. The melodic line is interrupted, yet the large arching phrase-mark bridges the rest during the phrase in question. This often demands of the performer a concentration of his expressive ability.

e) Motif rest

This leaves room for the 'negative copy' of a previous motif (for example, ♪|♫ 𝄾 𝄾 ♪|).

Harmony can be decisive for the significance of a rest in the following way:

a) Rests after chords of tension

These intensify the effect of chords. They often release an expectant mood, but often an anxious one, too.

b) Rests after special harmonic effects

These likewise intensify their effect.

c) Modulation rest

With this, the transition from one key to another occurs.

Dynamics are of great importance for the significance of a rest.

a) Rests after a ff

These are more easily drowned than:

b) Rests after a pp

Their effect thus depends on their length.

c) 'A rest during a crescendo passage

of a phrase increases the intensity ...

d) A rest in a diminuendo passage

detracts from the intensity.' (Riemann's *Lexikon*, under *Pause*).

In the form of a complete work there are four places where rests usually appear: at the beginning, at the end, at the transition, at the final cadence.

Now we have still to mention rests within part-writing.

a) Rests occurring in a voice line

These only have significance with an equal handling of the voices. In a large orchestral work, for example, longer periods of rest given to an instrument influence the timbre, of course, but are not experienced by the listener as rests.

b) Rests in the accompaniment

These are mostly bound up with the melody. That means the effect is less influenced by the accompaniment itself than by the melody lying above it, although the rest appears within the accompaniment.

c) Resolving rest

This appears during the change-over of the two voices or voice-complexes. When both partners are strongly differentiated we are dealing with an effect which we would like especially to look at as:

d) Echo rest

This belongs to what we might call 'filled-in rests'. To this we also have to include the effect occurring when:

e) A voice sounds on after a full orchestra ff

These points will now be developed with examples. It is perhaps not necessary to take all types into account and therefore only the most important will be chosen. The attempt to come closer to the phenomena of the rest from their usage by individual composers and to show the significance of the rest in different epochs of musical history appears to us more significant. (For further information see index on page 40, listing important examples for the special cases. It can be referred to during the reading of section 3.)

3) Examples from Musical Works

a) From the Baroque Period

An important phenomenon at the beginning of the baroque period is the strong dramatic tendency. New means were sought to fulfil this need. The rest acquired more and more significance; it was especially employed artistically in the setting of texts to music. The result Heinrich Schütz achieves in the *Easter Dialogue* (Example 1)[2] is quite astonishing. The change in the text occurs in the music too. Mary's anxiety that her Lord has been taken away to a place unknown to her makes her blind at first to the appearance of Christ. The music expresses this through its insistent flow of movement (beginning after ever-shortened rests on the main beats (a) which have an upbeat effect) during the previous intermittently repeated question of the angel ('woman, why weepest thou' and 'whom seekest thou'), connected at first to long notes. Just before the quoted passage, this question is also intensified through a semiquaver figuration. The stillness out of which Christ speaks to Mary, lifting her out of her anxiety so that she can recognize her Rabboni, is achieved musically through the rest (b) in which the movement changes from anxiety to stillness, the melodic flow changing to chords. The distinctive harmony deepens a second rest (c) in which the full awakening to the appearance of Christ occurs. The movement returns only after this recognition. Thus we feel the quiet measure of these bars as a transformation rest.

Schütz, from the *Osterdialog*   Example 1

We shall now explore the many more subtle sorts of rest, already in evidence with Schütz and during the succeeding time, in an outstanding figure who marked the last cornerstone of baroque music – J.S. Bach. By this, we should omit none of the all-important forms of the rest, since Bach is the most essentially representative composer of his epoch. We would rather achieve our aim adequately in the following observations by approaching at least a few significant personalities in the history of music.

Periods of rest are important for the texture of contrapuntal music. Rests temporarily illuminate and allow the separate voices to appear again more distinctly. They have special significance for the thematic entries in fugues. In Example 2, the theme is given prominence through the rest. The theme appears a second time in the tenor, in *stretto* with the theme in the soprano, and so could easily remain unobserved (a). At the same time the texture becomes lighter through the temporary silence in the alto (b).

From the A minor Fugue *(WTC 1)* Example 2

In instrumental music a rest appearing in *all* the voices together, the General Pause, only happens occasionally at the final cadence. The mostly uninterrupted movement of baroque music suddenly pauses on a chord, essential for the cadence (usually the dominant seventh chord). In our Example (2c from the same Fugue) the quaver movement sounds through the whole piece as the mediating unity. The sudden halt of this through the chord with a fermata produces in the following rest a deep inbreathing for a final increase of movement, which then comes to rest in the cadential bars. In chamber music and in orchestral works, but sometimes also in keyboard works, this rest is utilized for free improvisation by the soloist.

A further kind of rest, which is already used in the baroque era, is the *inner rest*. If we look at the quiet, uninterrupted line in the main theme of Bach's *Art of Fugue* (Example 3a) and compare it with its rhythmical variants, until rests finally intervene, then we can study the significance of the inner rest. It allows us to penetrate further into the melodic line which is at first almost unapproachable. You have the feeling that you could step out of yourself in these interruptions in order to grasp the event still more immediately. The whole work, which like a lofty annunciation approaches us ever closer, becomes particularly eloquent in Contrapunctus XI (Example 3b).

From the *Art of Fugue*
Theme from Contrapunctus I

Example 3
Theme from Contrapunctus XI

A characteristic of baroque music is the *adjacent placement of different levels:* f and p, *tutti* and *solo*, organ registration, etc., are changed to provide different or contrasting shades. Schütz already employed this means very drastically (for example, off-stage choirs). Echo effects which were produced in this way could be described as 'filled-out rests', that is, rests filled out with notes. The given level through the flow of a piece is suddenly interrupted and a distant effect claims our attention. As is always the case when a rest appears, here too we step out of ourselves and grasp the interrupted line from within with renewed activity (Example 4).

From the final chorus of *St Matthew Passion*   Example 4

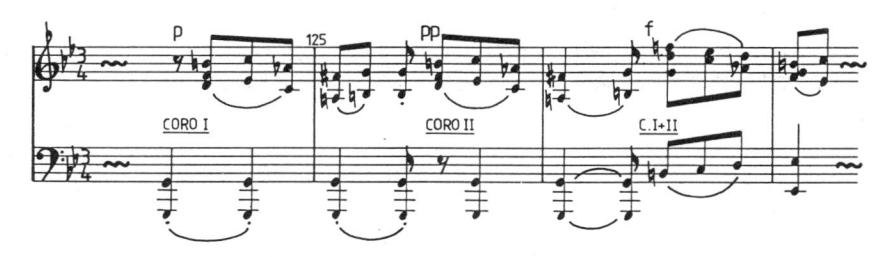

The use of two alternating choirs is also a means which satisfies the need for musical colouring. In the chorus No. 33 of Bach's *St Matthew Passion*, which we will discuss in detail later, this replacement is employed in the most differing degrees. One example is quoted here (Example 5). While with the echo effect of the gap we look into a deeper level of texture still appearing to us decisive, we arrive here through the constant change of choirs and rests to a regular or irregular alternation - each according to its placement in time.

From No. 33 of *St Matthew Passion* Example 5

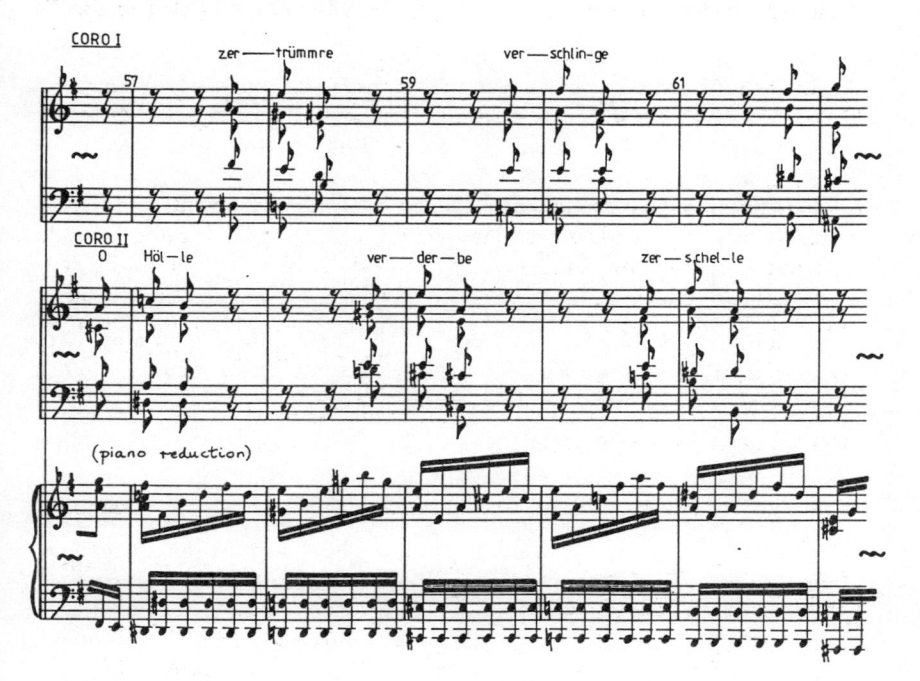

What we have observed now in detail, we find on a large scale too: the constituent parts of the *Passion* are also such adjacent levels. Recitative has the purpose of bringing the drama and the events of the gospels closer to the listener. He should be devoted completely to the words of the Evangelist. The rests between the short chords built up on top of each other strengthen the listener's attention, which is turned to the solo voice lying above or between them. How utterly different the effect is when Bach accompanies the words of Christ with sustained *chords in the strings*. We experience them as 'filled-in' rests, through which the soloist penetrates from a still deeper level. A mood of tranquillity and readiness is the result of these quiet resounding, static chords.

We experience another level in the mobility of the choruses (as already stated) and the arias. The accompaniment of the latter indicates interesting sorts of accompaniment rests which, however, in principle also appear in the classical period, and will be treated in that section.

Through the chorales the congregation is stimulated to a new level of being wakened up through its own activity. The breathing rest after the fermata for the choir and congregation (in other words all those assembled in the church) is the clearest expression not only in the music, but also in life and education, of an important occurrence.

Let us ask a question at this point, which is of great concern to the writer. If what follows helps towards gaining an answer, I cannot tell. An attempt should nevertheless be made. The question is: Through what means does Bach generate the unbelievable inner peace and composure which flows through us after hearing one of his works?

If we look at the above-quoted chorus No. 33 from the *St Matthew Passion*, we discover in bar 40 a General Pause with a fermata (Example b). It could have arisen initially from the two parts of the text. To the question, *'Sind Blitze, sind Donner in Wolken verschwunden?'* ('Will lightening and thunder in ruin engulf them?'), the answer follows, *'Eröffne den feurigen Abgrund o Hölle ...'* ('May Hell's fiery furnace in fury surround them ...').

From a musical point of view, however, Bach shows us in this rest something on a large scale which he continuously uses on a small scale.

The fugato-like theme at the beginning of the chorale (Example 6a) lasts for 4 bars and modulates from B minor to E minor. The answers of the entries do not follow in the dominant-tonic relationship, but in a continuous relationship of fifths. This gives a successive progression in the circles of fifths. After the entries of all four voices and an extra entry in the soprano, the keynotes on the circle of fifths return again in contrary motion, and so on.

Bach, from *St Matthew Passion* — Example 6

[Musical score: Vivace, with markings (a) at bar beginning and (b) at bar 40/41. Text underlay: "sind Blit—ze sind Don—ner in Wol—ken ver——schwunden sind .."]

We believe, with the help of our diagram, the following arrangement of Bach's harmony corresponds better than any other theoretical analysis, or one simply stating the degrees of the scale. We have listed the keynotes from F# to G in the order they appear on the circle of fifths, without considering whether they are related to either the major or the minor. Thus, in the first part of the chorus, an harmonic wave-like movement appears, which (in bars 31-35) passes through its deepest point in the faster changes of keynote in the four following bars, then it appears to reach out to G, then gently opens up to D, from there to reach to a still higher and mightier new beginning with full orchestra. It acquires the strength for this from the full bar's rest of bar 40 (Example 6b).

Hand in hand with the increasing steepness of this wave, the alternation of both choirs is speeded up. In bars 31-35 it reaches its climax: the words *'Blitze'* and *'Donner'* ('lightning' and 'thunder') cross in quick succession, which is

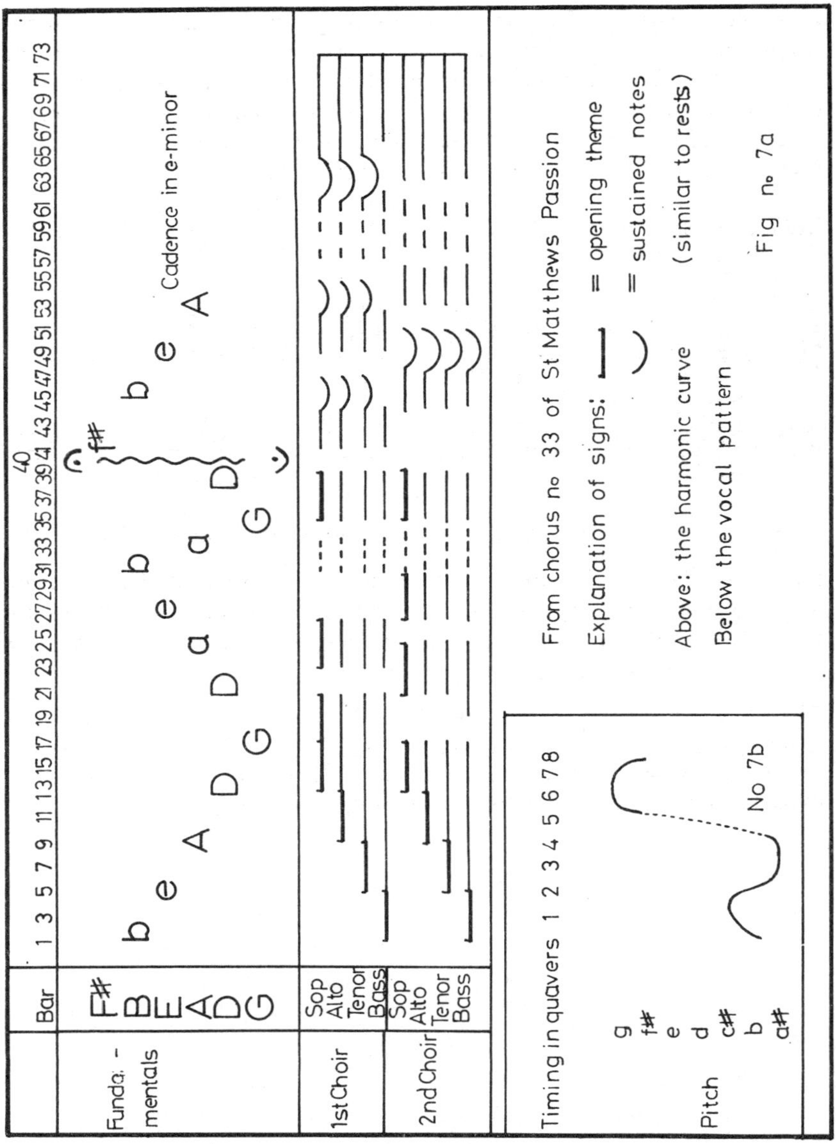

Example 7

From chorus no 33 of St Matthews Passion

Explanation of signs: ▬ = opening theme
) = sustained notes (similar to rests)

Above: the harmonic curve
Below: the vocal pattern

Fig no 7a

Fig no 7b

most dramatic. Their power supports the steep descent of the harmonic wave. And what of the General Pause that follows? It is a mighty pause for breath within a great wave-like movement. This health-giving taking in of breath, however, pervades all Bach's music. The movement is a constantly balanced, rhythmic swinging motion, which comes to expression as such in the smallest melodic line as in the largest harmonic sequence. The beginning of the soprano part of 'Blute nur, du liebes Herz' serves for an example of the former (Example 8): here too is a line which, after a steep descent (C# – A#), reaches up for a pause for breath (see analysis, Example 7b).

Bach, from *St Matthew Passion*   Example 8

[musical notation: No.12 Arie Coro II (piano reduction), Soprano, marked f]

Further evidence of this organic oscillation is Bach's use of ornamentation, and also the fact that large melodic leaps are never followed by similar leaps in the same direction; for example, an ascending octave leap is usually balanced by a movement downwards.

The health-giving breathing of Bach's music takes hold of us when listening. It is not 'breathless'; it contains that important rest which we have yet to speak of in the second part of this study, the 'breathing' rest. Through it we experience the inner tranquillity and gravity of the master.

b) Examples from the Classical Period

The stylistic upheaval which came with the transition from the baroque to the classical period is made very obvious in the kinds of rests and their use. The shading and contrasts which are achieved there through the lightening and thickening of the polyphonic texture and through the graded dynamics of *f* and *p*, *tutti* and *solo*, etc., gradually changed into the newly approaching *thematic contrast*. The human being of the baroque age created out of the unity of his being. Even where he depicts dramatic contrasts, he remains well grounded within himself. In the classical age, the contrasts were experienced even more inwardly (actually already anticipating the main problems of romanticism). The unity of form, which in baroque music rested on spinning around a single idea, with continuous support from the continuo, fell apart. In sonata form a second contrasting theme confronts the first theme. A bridge had to be constructed joining these contrasting ideas. This is for us the important element, the transition.

The great ABA form of the sonata was partially derived from the earlier *da capo* aria. Its middle section, however, became more and more the main part and centre of gravity which, with Beethoven (in the symphony, sonata, etc.), reached a certain peak of development. After a passing through foreign keys, often in conjunction with a contrapuntal working-out of the theme, the recapitulation grows out of the suspense of the middle section (the development) with a new clarity. A third phenomenon, which frequently appears in the classical period, was taken over from the French Suite: the slow introduction, which was to a certain extent a preparation leading on to the main content of the piece.

The rest in classical music, as in the baroque period, appears especially at the decisive points in the formal structure: in the introduction, the transition from first to second subjects, and in the development. The types of rests become more varied, their effects more forceful. A wealth of new examples of rests appears especially in Beethoven, which is connected with the whole ending of the classical era.

We will now bring two interesting phenomena from Ph. E. Bach, the representative of the pre-classical age. His sonatas are generally described as a preparation for classical sonata form. Even if the second subject seldom stands out clearly, the developments of his first movements are already close to a symphony of Haydn. Our example shows a detail from such a development (Example 9), from the collection *Für Kenner und Liebhaber*.

Ph. E. Bach
from Sonata IV, development section

Example 9

[musical notation]

A whole bar's rest follows the repeated motif in the bass taken from the main theme, with the interjections sounding above it. Its feeling of uncertainty is taken away by the *ff* which determines the new key. It is a kind of *rest of potentiality* as we often find it in the development of the classical sonata, but also in minuets and rondos, before the recapitulation of the main theme.

Ph. E. Bach, Rondo III

Example 10

[musical notation]

The second example (Example 10) is a rondo taken from the third book of the same collection. Here the main theme ends on a weak beat which reappears in the following bar after a crotchet rest. In the normal way this could be repeated once or twice more, to lead on as an upbeat and to continue once more in a regular pulse. Then the dynamics would have to remain unchanged. Ph. E. Bach, however, enlarges the crotchet rest in the following bar to a minim rest, instead of writing the expected note on the next beat, stretching it, so to speak; he thereby breaks the rhythmical flow as well as the *f*, and is able thus to continue with a *p* movement. For this rest, its relationship to the previous rhythmic note-values is essential. The change, however, is not only accomplished in dynamics and rhythm, but also in harmony. The last chord (E^b G) sinks deeper into our awareness through the lengthened rest and it is not difficult for us to transform its function from subdominant to dominant. During this rest we are lifted on to a new harmonic as well as dynamic level. The unexpected stretching changes it into a *transformation rest*.

From the many examples of rests in Haydn's symphonies, let us look at one from the last movement of his *Oxford Symphony* (Example 11). During the course of the development, the General Pauses repeatedly give us the feeling of insecurity and tension - similar to the first example from Ph. E. Bach. The last General Pause of this development is one full of promise: after passing through a final foreign key, the dominant seventh chord of the main key is reached and strengthened by a kind of echo from the flutes. The mood lightly, almost teasingly, anticipates the character of the main theme.

Haydn, 'Oxford' Symphony, from the 4th movement   Example 11

Mozart used the rest in a very subtle way. As Mersmann says, 'in places where the strongest power is generated, where a note, a release is expected, Beethoven "is silent" — and in reality Mozart is only symbolically silent at such moments' (Mersmann. *Musikästhetik*. Page 271). A phenomenon which we often find in Mozart is tellingly indicated here. Such a passage is found in the first movement of the first of the six quartets dedicated to Haydn, (Example 12a). The greatest drama is produced at the end of the bridge passage to the second subject by the syncopated *fp* of all four strings, together with the minor second passing-note in the cello. Suddenly, the three upper strings stop on a minim. If only a quaver were tied to this minim, and the movement were to move on further, then the connection to the previous syncopation would be retained. But, because a crotchet is tied, the halting of the movement is bridged over and the change to the uplifting p accomplished. (A similar case to Ph. E. Bach — Example 10.) The energy with which the movement is brought to a standstill is very striking to the listener, but it often presents difficulties for the players to bring it off (those who know the quartet will confirm this) (Example 12a).

Only after the movement is again brought to equilibrium does Mozart write a real rest on the last beat, through which the listener is gently led to the beginning of the second subject (Example 12b). This is once again a *breathing* rest. A second important, subtle rest appears in the coda before the last two bars. The upbeat element, running through the whole first part, is suddenly brought to a halt by the crotchet rest (Example 12c) and the movement commencing on the first beat of the bar comes to a standstill.

Mozart, from String Quartet in G major Example 12/1
(K. 387), first movement

We find *rests of direction* urging forwards in the development section. They fall on the first beat and, through their repetition, produce a syncopated effect (Example 12d).

Even in his operas, Mozart seldom employs full rests. They are mostly bound to words. Thus the tension in the exchange of words between Don Giovanni and the Comtur (in Act I of the opera) is intensified through a whole bar's rest. In *The Magic Flute,* longer rests appear in the introduction to the Overture, and — correspondingly — at the beginning of Act II, after the March of the Priests. In the latter case, the three fanfare-like calls of the priests are intensified by the three following rests, each one furnished with a fermata. The solemn assembly for prayer and the change to the supersensible is expressed through the rests between these chords. It is the decisive point of the opera: the trials of the two novices are prepared.

Example 12/2

[musical notation: Adagio, marked "(wind)"]

Example 13 shows a rest especially characteristic for arias, which somewhat corresponds to a cadential pause. The harmonic climax on the subdominant (sometimes also on the dominant seventh chord) is often prolonged through a fermata, leading on to the final cadence. In our example from the Introduction to *The Magic Flute* this fermata falls on a *rest*. The previous climax becomes highlighted through this in a very subtle way. Thus a transformation at the climax occurs in this rest.

The Three Ladies (from *The Magic Flute*, No. 1)   Example 13

[musical notation: (Allegretto) — "Sie wä—ren gern bei ihm al—lein, bei ihm al—lein, nein nein, nein nein"]

Let us now turn to that classical master whose music was the strongest expression of his inner feelings. Bach, still describing and creating from the inner peace and integrity of his being, presents contrasts to himself and to us. *Beethoven* now assimilates these contrasts, putting himself with his primeval strength between light and darkness, and creates from a continuous wrestling. We find this opposition of polar forces in larger forms as in the smallest details. And again, as with Bach, we seek the primeval creative force, where Beethoven brings the tremendous stream of his music to a halt. Where he is turned completely to the light we find the in-breathing of the inner being come to rest, too. With Bach this inner peace is the *starting point* for his creating, whereas for Beethoven it is the *goal*.

Beethoven employed the *accompaniment rest* more diversely than all the composers before him. We shall now discuss this.

In the opening theme of the first movement of the *Piano Sonata in F minor*. op. 2/1, the ascending line (bar 2), divided by non-legato rests, reaches its climax (Example 14). The similarly shortened accompaniment chords begin after this climax as upbeats, and end in the next bar (bar 3) in which, at the same time, the main theme makes a fresh start. After this second climax the accompaniment begins again, from now on, however, ending with a rest on the first beat, with which the main theme also falls, and with the upbeat shortened to a grace note. The *whole melodic line* reaches its climax in bar 7 and sinks down on to a fermata rest. The accompanying chords are completely determined by the dynamic of the first theme. For them, the rests on the downbeat are *rests of potentiality*: the accompaniment receives the impulse from the top voice in order to enhance it. Through the division of the motifs these syncopated *rests of potentiality* appear with increased frequency and reinforce the forward urge of the theme. We understand the fermata rest if we view the accompaniment chords as upbeats. From bar 5 they break into the ever stronger accented beginnings of the main theme, finally to reach into the emptiness of the fermata rest. The impulsive strength sinks back on to itself. It is then possible to work up to a new start after a complete relaxation.

Beethoven, op. 2/1   Example 14

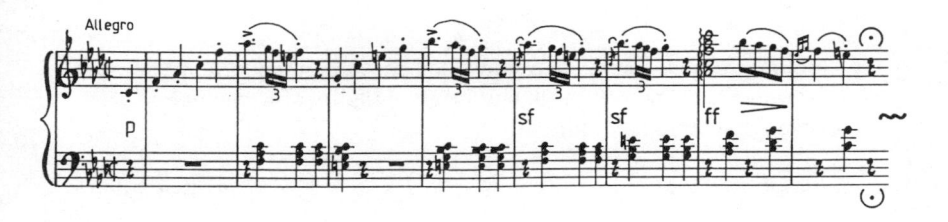

The second movement of the *String Quartet*, op. 18/1 in F major begins with muted accompaniment of the three lower strings (Example 15a). The tension of these almost lifeless chords placed next to each other arises, above all, through the *non-legato rests*, which appear especially clearly in pp. We have the case here of a rest being especially felt through the restrained dynamic. It is clear to me from two observations that the effect of these rests is not to be underestimated. The intensity with which a concert audience gives itself over to what is being presented is substantially enhanced through such short interruptions. Movements and noises in the audience often start spontaneously *after* such passages, which had claimed its whole attention. Similarly, I have succeeded as a pianist for eurythmy (an art of movement) in bringing children, who were often restless and unconcentrated at the start of a lesson, to listen especially through such a lightening up of the melodic line. An absolute *legato* playing would have stimulated them to a still greater restlessness. Brighter playing — especially supported by a *pp* — awakens them to the music.

In our Example 15a these *non-legato rests* become *rests of potentiality* which prepare the expansive phrase of the upper part, and later allow it to come out clearly.

We have noted an exhilarating example in Example 15b. Here, too, the *rests of potentiality* direct the attention of the listener to the soaring melody above.

Beethoven, from String Quartet op. 18/1   Example 15

Beethoven, Symphony No. 1, second theme from the 1st movement

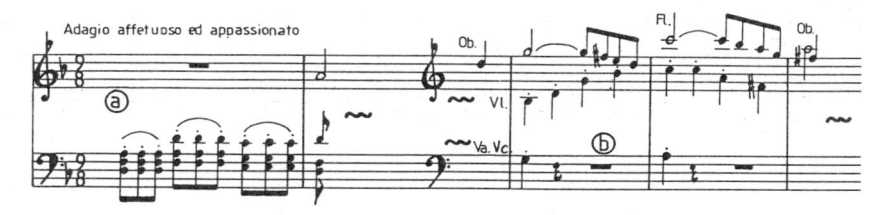

In the melody, such a change of note-values appears in the form of *phrasing rests* (Example 16). The lifting up and brightening up after the phrase-mark brings breath to the melodic line.

From Symphony No. 1   Example 16

Another interesting phenomenon, especially employed by Beethoven, is the *motif rest*. In our Example 17a the rest which corresponds to the opening motif appears like the negative of an answer. Only later is the answer really given. Riemann notices that, according to Beethoven's own comments, 'the three introductory notes signify a question put to a melancholic person, as to whether he is still melancholic' (*Analyse von Beethovens Klaviersonaten.* Book 1. Page 372). With this we have at the same time the interesting example of a *rest at the beginning*. Beethoven, like so many other great people, often had to suffer greatly from the insensitivity of his fellow men for what moved him. Nothing annoyed him more than the inattention of the listener. Beethoven shakes the listener awake still more strongly when he begins a work with strong chords broken up by rests. It is not only the sudden *forte* that contributes to this effect. Imagine the beginning of the *Eroica* (Example 17b) with sustained dotted minims instead of short crotchet beats! It is just these rests which prepare the listener for the beginning of the first theme in bar 3.

Rondo, from op. 10/3   Example 17

Allegro con brio, from the 'Eroica'

In a similar way, Beethoven's works (as other classical masters' too) often end with chords interspersed with rests. And it is interesting to observe when Beethoven places a fermata over the last, often whole bar's, rest (for example, *Pathetique Sonata*, first movement). What does he mean by this? These decisive rests, shown by Beethoven, we will discuss in the second part of this study.

The Funeral March of the *Eroica* contains a wealth of different types of rest. Part of this movement for strings beginning in E^b major, quoted in Example 18, is covered by a large dynamic phrase-mark. With the upbeat of the first violins, a heightening effect commences, which, through shortening rests, is lightened up and brought out. The intensification, after reaching the uncertain diminished seventh chord, is led over to a rest, to end in a sudden cry on the dominant seventh chord, determining the minor key, and sinks back again in a transition rest extended through the slow tempo. This transformation rest is an example of the demands which Beethoven often makes on the player. How difficult to span over this long-lasting rest! In such rests especially we become aware whether the interpretive artist is equal to the work.

From the 2nd movement of the 'Eroica' Example 18

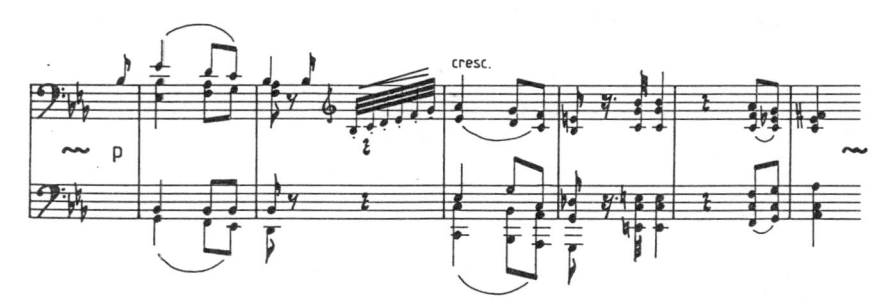

A *transition rest* from the same movement is quoted in Example 19a. The *crescendo* on the descending D^b major arpeggio, brought out by the non-legato rests of the strings in unison, suddenly breaks off, *piano*, on the leading-note of C minor. The oppressive silence after this unexpected harmonic and dynamic event prepares us for the reappearance of the main theme.

From the 2nd movement of the 'Eroica' Example 19

At the end of this movement we can see the significance of the downbeat. Here, with the turning towards the major, a strong predominance on the main beat is connected through syncopated rests and ties. The phrases of the violins, held in pp, wander like flickering shadows in the heights (Example 19b). The following, opposite effect is intensified still further in this: already the descending line of violins and flutes is lit up through non-legato rests (here we have the example of a pause of direction in *decrescendo*). This, however, ends in a muffled pp timpani beat (Example 20). Through this breaking off of the melody, as we would like to say, only the pulse remains. We receive the impression of being pulled forcefully into the depths. The fragmented phrases of the theme, which now follow, are accompanied further by these muffled beats. After a final build-up, a complete relaxation appears.

From the 2nd movement of the 'Eroica' Example 20

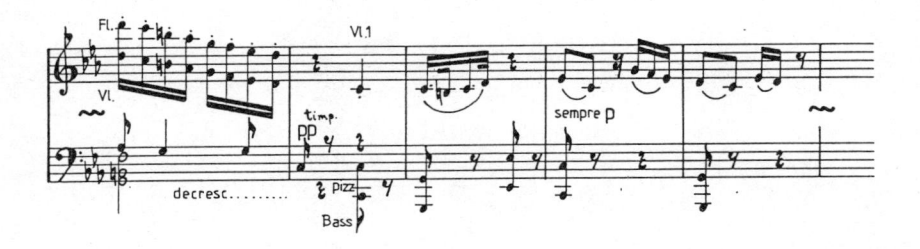

With Beethoven we can see the contrasts referred to above still more clearly in his *Fifth Symphony*.

Fifth Symphony Example 21

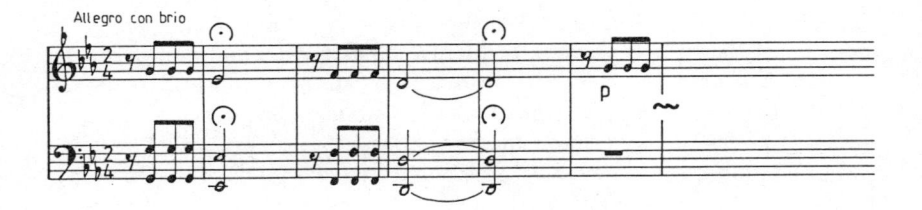

The rests which occur after the fermata of the violent opening motif (Example 21) bear the character of a beginning rest. The impetuous urging forward of the whole movement is repeatedly released through a rest on the downbeat of the main theme, where this urge culminates in a climax. Beethoven breaks up the flow through the use of *rests of intensification* and *transition*. These points are in the exposition of the second repetition of the opening motif, in the transition to the second subject, and at the end before the recapitulation commences. In them, at the same time, the precipitous opening motif comes temporarily to rest.

Beethoven reaches the highest inner dynamic, after an oppressive four bars of tension of a diminished seventh chord, through a sudden silence (Example 22). After the releasing effect of the first inversion of the dominant chord, we turn downwards again and are caught up by the introductory horn call of the second subject. Beethoven leads us at this point to the edge of what is physically possible. In the rest, for a moment, he lets us divine regions lying beyond this threshold.

From the 1st movement of the 'Eroica'   Example 22

The second movement stands in contrast to this. The glorious moving melodic phrases are lifted, after deeply inhaled breathing pauses, leading us confidently to the heights of the brilliant *fortissimi*. After the ending which is lit up by shortening rests — as after a long outbreathing — such a phrase begins afresh on a weak beat (Example 23a). This strange appearance of the main theme from the first movement does not appear at the climax but before it, in a subdued *piano*, and allows, for a moment, the wonderful breathing motion of this movement to be paralysed (Example 23b). However, it is only like a pause before drawing in a new breath.

From the 2nd movement of the Fifth Symphony   Example 23

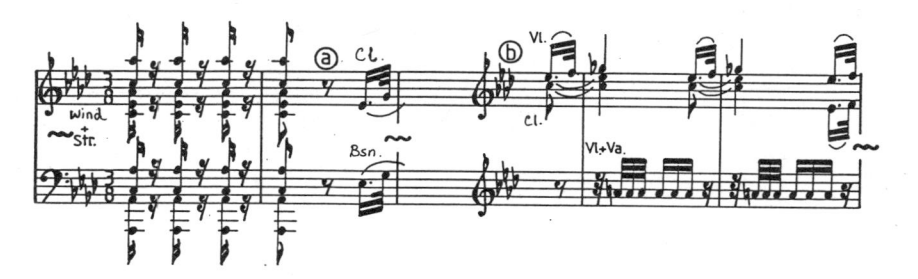

The creeping motion of the introduction to the third movement now steps out of an impenetrable depth and begins again after a breathing rest (Example 24a). Only in the forward-moving main theme is the middle reached between the heights of the first movement and the depths from which the mysterious introduction appears. The opening theme of the first movement, which felt so urgent because of the rests on the main beat, has now been transformed (Example 24b). The rests between the chords of the accompanying strings create the space for this middle region.

From the 3rd movement of the Fifth Symphony   Example 24

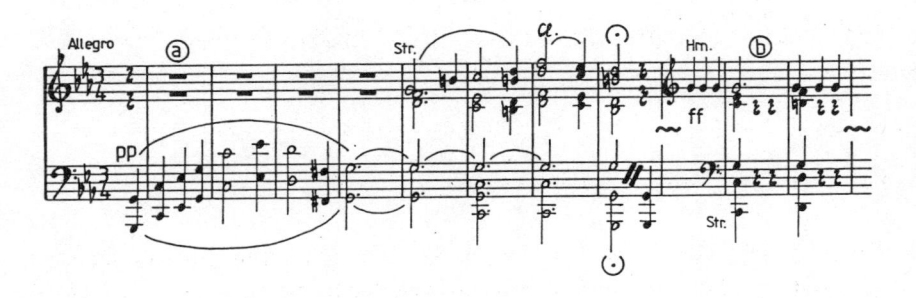

After the trio-like middle section of this movement, rests have a subverting effect by splitting up, all of a sudden, both of the reappearing themes. The line is broken up from within. A subdued *pp* increases the effect of this rest (Example 25).

From the 3rd movement of the Fifth Symphony   Example 25

We already sense in it a mighty transformation process. With the interrupted cadence on A^b this section goes into the transition which is as effective as hardly any other expression of the ungraspable could be (Example 26). We arrive at the lower reaches of the sense-perceptible in *ppp*. The frozen chords of the strings allow us to feel the emptiness of space, and the muffled beat of the timpani is like a final dull show of life that, quietly waiting, accompanies this transition. Is it not like a groping towards a nameless nothingness? Outwardly it is so, yet we perceive clearly the great transformation which occurs inwardly in this process of dissolution. Into the held breath of this rest of potentiality, the new impetus can get to work, which creates the last movement.

Beethoven, transition to the 4th movement of the 5th Symphony Example 26

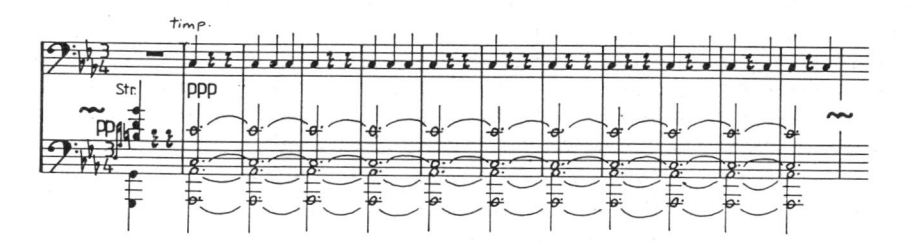

'In all transitions, as an in-between region, a higher spiritual power appears to want to break through,' said Novalis. And we understand, too, when Beethoven, before the recapitulation in the last movement, once again enters that in-between region. We can understand him through what Novalis expresses in the following words:

'This, however, is the great secret, the eternal unfathomable: Out of pain the new world is born and ash dissolved in tears will become the draught of eternal life. However, the heavenly Mother is living in everyone, in order to give birth to this eternal Child. Oh — do you not feel, beating in your breasts, the growing of the New?'

c) Examples from the Romantic Era

With the later works of Beethoven, the development of music has already paved a way to the peaks of romanticism via the early romantic, Schubert. Only with difficulty can we reduce this epoch in musical history to a common denominator. Ernst Kurth made a general comment in his book on Bruckner (page 9): 'Coming from this classical attitude, the romantics, drunk with secrets, sought again to stand on ground lying nearer the darker regions; not this itself, not their own fundamental basis, became the actual standing ground, but a region of twilight that unites light and dark in a particular, characteristic way; only to roam out from here in the face of complete darkness and complete light.' What with Beethoven was only *transition* from darkness to light, becomes now the *point of departure* and the dualism, which Beethoven still managed to overcome through his strong individual personality, became for humanity an unbridged chasm. The striving for unity in form resulted from the need to make real, externally, what was no longer achieved within by the romantic person. With Schubert this does not yet appear so strongly. Standing at the threshold from classicism to romanticism, he strove in the wrestling for form (especially in the instrumental works) still harking back to Beethoven. Thus Moser says that 'from the first, he was cut out to be an incomparable writer of Lieder, also later as a master of instrumental music, though he first had to achieve maturity gradually through strict self-discipline' (*Musikgeschichte*. Page 225).

Through the rests in the first movement of the *Unfinished Symphony*, Schubert appears to want forcefully to tear himself and his listeners from being carried away by the wonderful song-like second theme. The effect of the rest is completely different in the recapitulation from that in the exposition. The second subject consists of two phrases (see Example 27). The first is of four bars and begins on the tonic. The second, lengthened phrase leads through a deviation to the supertonic in the fifth bar, and back to the main key. The ending should follow in the sixth bar, that is, the tenth bar of the whole theme. With the first appearance in the cellos, this concluding bar coincides with the violins in the restatement of the theme. In the *exposition*, however, this repeat ends in a whole bar's rest (Example 27a).

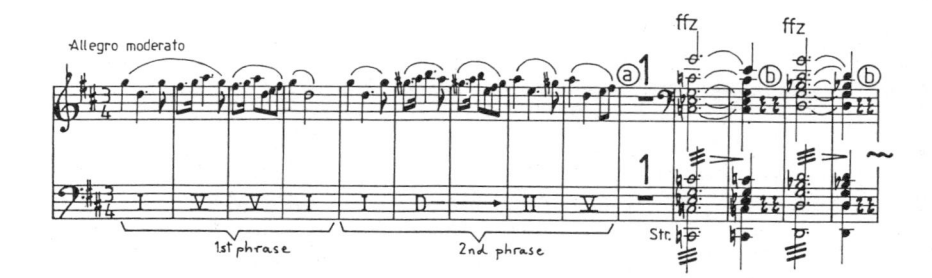

Schubert, from the 1st movement of the B minor Symphony   Example 27

The modulation returning to the tonic is accomplished, having arrived at its dominant; only the final chord is still missing. The listener, completely given up to this wondrous theme, gradually wakes up. The harmonic sequence has indeed almost reached its full relaxation. Hardly realizing what is happening, the outburst of a mighty orchestral *ff* storms over the listener, the logical outcome of the unfinished theme. Only in the rest after this first outburst (Example 27b) and its repeat on the 6/4 chord of the tonic minor, does the listener grasp the situation again.

How different in the recapitulation! Here, *before* the General Pause, a very remarkable phenomenon occurs. The theme is played this time in D major firstly by the cellos, then repeated by the violins to reach the tonic again after the deviation to the supertonic (E minor), but continuing this stepwise downward movement, it reaches, after C major, the dominant of B minor (Example 28). The *decrescendo* and the chromatic downward sliding of the accompanying instruments (clarinet and bassoon) strengthen the effect. The uncomfortable feeling of being suddenly left to fall after the melodious theme has carried him down, awakens the listener here. The rest has a redeeming and activating effect. In it the listener catches up after wandering off, and moves *himself* towards the *ff* outburst. However, he now reaches for the sombre B minor too, which is arrived at again with great conviction through the inner activity thus awakened.

Schubert, from the 1st movement of the B minor Symphony   Example 28

The frequent use of syncopation, especially in Brahms and Schumann, often leads to interesting appearances of rests: the sections in *Fast zu ernst* from *Kinderscenen (Scenes from Childhood)*, containing running semiquaver movement, find their ending each time in a chord which is tied over from the semiquaver movement already prepared in the previous bar (Example 29a). The stopping of the movement shortly before the new bar creates the effect of a *mainbeat rest*: it is a taking hold of the chord which sounds on.

Similar to Example 29b: the cutting short of the sounding of the accompaniment at the end of the F# major *Romanze* (op. 28/3) allows us to experience the ending in the rest, that is, to experience the held notes, now clearly coming to the fore because of the rest.

Schumann   Example 29

From 'Fast zu ernst', op. 15/10   Ending of the Romanze, op. 28/2

We see still more strongly the effect of the rest as a negative note-value in Example 30, from the second movement of Brahms's *A major Violin Sonata*. The rests are understood from the iambic motif (a), upon which the whole *Vivace* is based. The prominence of the unstressed second beat is retained in the concluding bars. The forwards-urging character of the iambus (u —), however, is conditioned by the concentrated short foot. The strict movement of this section comes to an end, making possible the return to the *Andante*, through the short feet being first shortened (b), then stopped (c), at the same time through the *diminuendo* (rest of direction). The rest here does not stop the flow of the movement before the ending (as so often) but blots out the first beat of the bar, finally becoming the negative of the short iambic foot.

Brahms, from the 2nd movement of the Violin Sonata in A major Example 30

These phenomena with Schumann and Brahms, with which we so clearly have the sense of being lifted out of ourselves, become artificially used up in jazz. Here, on the other hand, it wants to be controlled and is only used sparingly with the aim of preparing for the reception of the positive movement of what follows — this very means is employed in jazz for its own sake.

Brahms, from the 1st movement of Symphony No. 4   Example 31

We experience in the first movement of the *E minor Symphony* the particular twilight in which romanticism likes to live. After the second subject, Brahms leads us into the opaque dusk of the diminished seventh chord, he hints at a motif played on the trumpets which we know already from the beginning of the second subject (Example 31). This mysterious twilight ceases after four bars. After a short rest the fanfare call is heard three times before it proceeds further. This short motif acquires clear contours through the rest and now comes out distinctly in contrast to the previous hazy or indistinct background. The rest here disperses the sombre appearance and creates a new deep effect and a clarity.

With this example we arrive now at the great symphonist of romanticism: Anton Bruckner. We find this twilight in Bruckner at places where he sinks back after a 'symphonic wave' (Kurth). Yet, for him, this between-stage is not a means to reach new clarity, as it was for Brahms: for Bruckner it is only transition. We find this unique sombreness in the *Fourth Symphony* at the end of the exposition in the chromatic, downwards-gliding seventh chords (Example 32a).

Bruckner, from the 1st movement of Symphony No. 4   Example 32

Passing through this we arrive at the stillness from which Bruckner, both as a human being and as a composer, starts out. The almost inaudible sound of the drumroll vibrates through space. And just because of this the rest becomes especially strong. It becomes a *rest of potentiality* from which something new can grow.

For Bruckner, the rest is an important means of expression. For him, as he is reported to have said (Kurth. Page 376), it is 'an intake of breath'. In his symphonies, the transition between each individual theme is often interspersed with whole-bar rests (because of this, his *Second Symphony* was nicknamed the *Rest Symphony*), or is pervaded by a single voice, appearing like a filled-out rest after a mighty orchestral *ff*. Thus, the transition to the third theme in the *Fourth Symphony* occurs in two bars of transition rests heard on the horns (Example 32b). The third theme itself belongs to those wonderfully translucent melodies, whose free breathing quality is what we enjoy in Schubert.

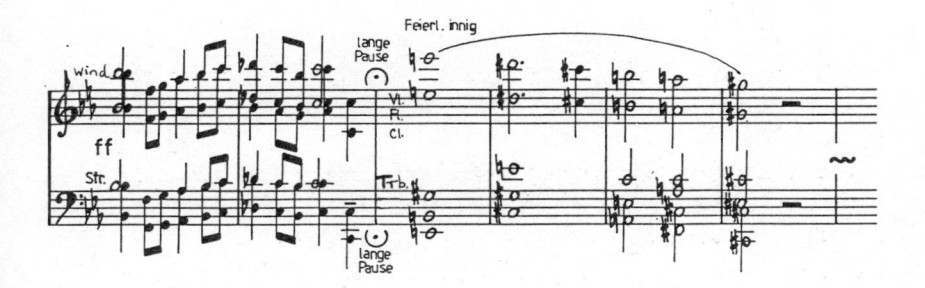

Bruckner, from the 4th movement of the 8th Symphony   Example 33

Absolute rests are stronger still than the filled-out rests. We find one in the finale of the *Eighth Symphony* (Example 33). In the third theme, the four-bar unison, which gradually increases towards the full orchestral *ff*, suddenly breaks off on a fermata placed on the bar line: as in a quiet transformation, we are led to the eight-bar, hymn-like transition theme. This unique episode is like the self-possession and devotional composure of a religious person: we clearly recognize therein the creator of the work.

With this we would like to conclude our musical observations. It has already been explained why we refrain from including many composers contemporary with those quoted. From opera we have only quoted from *The Magic Flute*, since the whole development of opera is but dimly illuminated by a discussion on types of rest. Of course, examples are not lacking there, yet these are either bound to words, or where not, they are mostly very similar to the examples taken here from the respective period.

4) Index of Examples

1. Rhythmic:
   a) Rests on the strong beat: 1a, 12d, 14, 21, 29a.
   b) Rests on the weak beat: 12b, 23a.
   c) Shortening rests: 23a.
   d) Non-legato rests: 14, 15, 32.
   e) Connection to the previous rhythmical note-values: 10.
   f) Sustained notes: 12a, 26.

2. Melodic:
   a) Phrasing rest: 16.
   b) Breathing rest: 6, 8, 12b, 23.
   c) Interruption of a melodic phrase: 20.
   d) Inner (built-in) rest: 30.
   e) Motif rest: 17a.

3. Harmonic:
   a) Rests after chords of tension: 11, 18, 19a 22.
   b) Rests after special harmonic sequences: 10.
   c) Modulation rest: 1b, 10, 32b, 33.

4. Dynamic:
   a) Rest after *ff*: 17b, 22.
   b) Rest after *pp*: 19a, 22.
   c) Rest during a *crescendo*: 18, 19a.
   d) Rest during a *diminuendo*: 20, 30.

5. Form:
   a) Initial rests: 17, 21.
   b) Ending rests: 17, 29b.
   c) Transition rests: 11, 19a, 22, 26 32b.
   d) Cadential rests: 2b.

6. Part-Writing:
   a) Rest in a voice line: 2a.
   b) Rests in the accompaniment: 14, 15, 24b.
   c) Resolving rest: 5.
   d) Echo rest: 4.
   e) A voice sounding on after a full orchestral *ff*: 33b.

Transformation rests: 1b, 10, 12/2, 13, 18, 22, 26, 32b, 33.

Rests of direction: 12d, 18, 19a, 20, 22, 30.

Rests of potentiality: 9, 14, 15, 17b, 19, 32a.

REFERENCES

1   Suggestions for the observations for these types I discovered in Riemann's reference book (under *Pause*). My chosen expressions do not all correspond with Riemann's.

2   Heinrich Schütz, *Osterdialog nach Johannes 20: 13,16 und 17*, for four solo voices and continuo.

II THE REST IN LIFE AND EDUCATION

1) Nature and the Human Being

The whole of nature pulsates with the most diverse rhythms. Every organism has its own rhythm. It is subject to the rhythmical influences from the environment and at the same time itself affects the rhythm of other organisms. The change from day to night, from summer to winter, ebb and flow, the regular fluctuation in air pressure, the winds, terrestrial magnetism, the breath, digestion and growth processes; these and all the other natural phenomena occur in certain rhythms. In the low point of the rhythmical curve, however, between relaxation and renewed tension, between exhaling and inhaling, between death and coming into being, a (more or less long) anti-climax, or point of rest is included, in which nature begins a new movement, developing renewed force. The rest, which we have studied in music, has a similar significance in nature.

The human being lives surrounded and pervaded by these phenomena. He, like other organisms, has his own rhythm, too. The tendency to emancipate himself from the surrounding influences is especially strong with him. He can oppose them by his own healthy activity. He also has the ability, however, so to alter the conditions of his life that he is threatened to become enslaved by the development he himself has evoked. Movements in mankind's history repeatedly appear under the motto, 'back to nature', wishing to renounce this so-called advance. In spite of them, the unnaturalness of civilization develops repeatedly. Illnesses appear as a result. Consequently, the unrest and instability of our life today has the effect of damaging the health of the human organism. Art and education can, by stimulating the inner counter-forces in the human being, work together in the process of healing this sickness of civilization. They can contribute generally to regaining a higher level which we have lost: our relationship to the healing forces of nature.

2) Enthusiasm and Discipline

Enthusiasm and discipline are the premises of all art. Enthusiasm, the highest and noblest drive of man, creates ever anew in the stream of artistic work. However, 'discipline is the word in which the new man can find himself' (Christian Morgenstern). It accumulates and concentrates inner initiatives; it shapes and forms; it checks and restrains the course of development.

The balance and the stimulation of both these polar forces is the task of the artist. Just as uncontrolled enthusiasm would impel us to boundless fantasy, so discipline without enthusiasm would lead to miserable philistinism.

The rest is a phenomenon that is determined by both forces. If discipline is its main component, it would be absurd without enthusiasm. This becomes checked in the rest, but it also becomes regenerated. Thus, from the beginning, we emphasize that the rest be inserted into the flow of an event. It must be actively formed or felt. Only in the alternating play of both these forces does it have the significance which we ascribe to it.

3) The Breathing Rest as Expression of Inner Calm

'Human qualities are only developed in calmness. Without this, love loses the power of its truth and its blessing' (*Schwanengesang*. Page 286). With these words, Pestalozzi leads us to a basic problem of early education. The sources of unrest, as he then explains, are want and suffering. Their consequences are lovelessness and disbelief, and what is connected with them. A widespread picture of our time! Pestalozzi makes the mother responsible for the peace of the child, in which 'human qualities can develop'. Yet when he goes on, that she should do everything to 'promote this calm and prevent any disturbance' (Page 563), then the question arises: How far is this at all possible for mothers today? How often are they no longer able to create this necessary atmosphere for the child.

How we can take pains to help mothers will be indicated in the next section but one. Let us now ask ourselves how this calmness of the grown-up is passed over to the child. We have already suggested the answer above, with Bach. In observing the breathing rest through his harmonious breathing, the educator allows calmness to stream out. His actions, his walk, his words, his gestures are determined by his measured breathing. The musician, too, should be able to accomplish this. In the concert hall he can give back to the listeners what they have lost through this separation from nature. This capacity is even more important for the music teacher. He has to be conscious during singing that the children learn to feel the breathing rests in the rhythmical swing of the song; that he himself intervenes, in order to avoid any possible agitation, hurrying or jostling, and to lead the children to a calm breathing, to living but controlled movement. Then his lesson acquires the meaning which is often overlooked: the healing of restlessness.

The young person, however, who is thus educated 'has within himself higher claims of the mind and heart, which he strives for with serious intent, considered calmness and inner quiet' (op. cit. Page 569).

4) The Variety of Phenomena

> Dem grossen Meister in dem Reich der Töne,
> Der nie zu wenig tat und nie zuviel,
> Der stets erreicht, nie überschritt sein Ziel,
> Das mit ihm eins und einig war: das Schöne!
>
> To the great master in the realm of sound,
> Who never did too little nor too much,
> Who always reached his goal — not overstepping it
> Beauty agreed with him and was one with him!

With the above lines Franz Grillparzer ends his poem, 'Mozart' (see Erich Valentin. *Wege zu Mozart*. Page 185). Beauty springs from the heart of him who could remain measured. It originates in the law of measure, in nature!

How difficult it often is for us to strive for this! We easily allow ourselves to be carried away on the comfortable, lethargic stream of the everyday, without any idea of what things we are missing. And how often do we allow ourselves to be chased by the above-mentioned unrest due to technology, without realizing any of the manifold wonders lying at our feet. We have to bring to rest the restlessness as well as the indolent drifting about. And if we do not have the strength to do so, we have to practise it in small as well as big things. The teacher himself especially has to work towards it.

But is it not enough, that we have the means today of surrounding ourselves with the diversion of uninterrupted 'entertainment'? We have no desire here to discuss its value, yet the influence, for example, which the radio exerts, when it accompanies the course of the day for some people as continuous background noise, should not be overlooked, especially with children, who are not yet able to protect themselves from their surroundings. They become so used to what bombards their ears, that they only half listen or actually not at all, instead of becoming sensitive to the world's subtleties.

Let us recall what we developed with the *inner rest*. The melodic line is interrupted. We approach it closer, grasp it so to speak from within, more immediately and with considerable activity. And thus we should hold on to it in life and in education! Not in order to divide it up, but to experience the flow of events more strongly from within, to differentiate, and indeed to combine polarities.

What do we admire so much in an experienced teacher? That he knows well how to use the subtle effects of the rest. When he suddenly stops after a lively presentation, or carries on softly; when he interrupts before the climax, thus intensifying its effect; by these means he will always gain the attention and alertness of the children. A teacher must, to a certain degree, control rests as a means to an end in his delivery. The rest, moreover, is also useful for the restoration of discipline. Does it not have a concentrating effect when a teacher is able to bring the tumult of a class to a halt with a gesture! Here a rest can be more effective than violent shouting. Restlessness can only be stopped through calmness. The 'brightening rest', as we have already shown with musical examples, is also able to lead the pupil to renewed attention.

But what else is lack of discipline than a sleepiness regarding the rich abundance of phenomena? Young people should learn to experience the variety and colourfulness of nature. As Adalbert Stifter points out, the senses have first to be attuned to the fine differentiations, something which enlivens Mozart's music so splendidly. This needs to be cultivated. It is not possible if (speaking metaphorically) we dash about in the world with machines. It is only achieved when we know how to remain on our own path.

Each greater completed period of time should commence with a rest and end with a rest. The *initial* and *final rests* are life's great *rests of transition*. We have shown with Beethoven, for example, how he writes rests after the opening chords of the *Eroica*, thus engaging the listener. Yet does the initial rest play a lesser role in Bach? Bach just has not written it in. Perhaps the age in which he lived was more receptive. Do we not experience a work much more intensely if, like some conductors, we concentrate ourselves in a short silence before its commencement, to raise ourselves, as it were in a 'transition rest', from the previous everyday level to the level of the work of art! The impression of a work is deepened if we let it finish with a final rest in order to make its full effect, and to take it with us into everyday life.

An artist of life has the skill to resist the danger of hastening in blind restlessness from one activity to another. He would much rather begin something new with fresh strength after a short rest for contemplation.

Children should learn the art of living. Accordingly every teacher should be an artist. He or she will create the initial rest afresh each time like an artist, so that it does not appear as something tedious or ridiculous to the children. He will receive and collect a rowdy class, for example, with a shared activity or with some suitable words, in order then to direct their activity through a short rest towards the content of the lesson. I tried myself in a recorder group with some eight-year-olds to help them concentrate at the beginning of their lessons by drawing their attention to some noise in the adjacent room, thus, at the same time, letting them sense the quietness of their own room. If it succeeded, the lesson acquired content and life.

What we only achieve through our own efforts is found as a law in nature. Do we not make for ourselves such a natural 'transition rest' when we sleep? Our forces acquire new strength. And how often on the following day do we achieve what we tried to do in vain the previous day! And if we now look at the sleep which a seed passes through before it is able to germinate, and the hibernation of some animals, do we not have the finest examples of how the change to new strength, to greater and more manifold vitality appears in the rest?

5) Readiness: the Basis for Mutual Understanding and the Source of Inner Calm

Two types of activity exist: one is positive and is directed outwards. With it we mean everything which we simply call activity. The other is negative (not the bad sense) and consists in an 'emptying of ourselves'. It is *readiness*. In *rests of direction* and *transformation rests* we clearly perceive a force which demands something specific. They are inserted into the dynamic movement. In the *rest of readiness*, on the other hand, we stop within, without asking whether anything is happening. The inner dynamic also finds rest here. In the previous section, we suggested how children can be led to experience the quietness in a room. This being 'wholly ear', this perceiving the room, is 'readiness'.

Is not the calmness in a class remarkable when the teacher has still to get things ready, or to give them out, and only the rustling of paper or the step of a pupil is audible? Everything is in a state of expectation. The teacher should not lose such suspense too soon. He should perceive it as the necessary attitude of the class towards him, in so far as he is the active one. He can perceive it while he speaks, too. He is only obliged to give the necessary balance to this readiness through what he has to bring. Similarly with the concert artist; he, too, can have this remarkable experience of the audience's inner readiness. He has to perceive it at those moments when his playing, for example, goes into a sustained pp passage or even when he pauses altogether during a rest. Through this, he becomes one with the audience. He can feel whether giving and receiving reciprocate.

A concert can sometimes appear to us as lacking in atmosphere. In most cases the artist was not able to awaken the necessary expectancy in his audience. But it is also possible that the audience is not willing to take anything in, despite the presence of the greatest artist (for example, the audience may be unable to overcome its preconceptions). Let us recall the letter in which the twenty-two-year-old Mozart tells his father about the visit to Madame La Duchesse de Chabot. The 'miserable piano' upon which he had to play and the freezing room offended him much less than the guests who carried on drawing, paying no attention to him. 'If you give me the best piano in Europe with an audience which understands nothing, or does not want to understand and which do not feel with me in what I am playing, I shall lose all pleasure ...' (Paris 1 May 1778).

It is a task of music lessons to practise this 'being ready for audible impressions' (we do not mean only aural training, which is nevertheless an essential part of it). Its aim is not limited to educating the members of an audience to be as good as they possibly can. Much rather is it meant to waken in the children the ability to listen at all. We can imagine that the part-song can contribute to this. While the one group of children is actively singing, the other should be made attentive by the teacher to practise active readiness. If the teacher, through his correct attitude, is able to bring about for some moments a 'rest of readiness' with the children, then much is accomplished. The seed of an important social element has been sown: listening to the other when meeting someone; being able to relinquish our own opinion, which often appears so important, and to step towards the other without expectation, without personal criticism. Young people should learn to achieve this. Later on they will experience those beautiful moments in which people try to understand each other instead of *disagreeing*. For the finest experience of a relationship of person to person is conversation.

The 'rest of readiness' is the holding back of our own personality in order to create space for something else. We take in musical sounds and words. We can also tune in to the quietness of the space. Sometimes this quietness comes upon people at the most important turning points of their lives. How simply Selma Largerlöf describes such a turning point in her story *The Girl from the Marsh Croft*:

> Gudmund stopped for a while in the middle of the courtyard and listened for footsteps. It was completely still, not a breath of air moved. He thought never before had he experienced such stillness. It was as if the whole forest held its breath, standing there and waiting for something extraordinary to happen.

Some people are afraid of this silence. They always want to be surrounded by noise. Others, however, seek it out. For them quietness becomes readiness, the source of inner peace. What the former miss, what the latter seek, Meister Eckhart tells us:

> We listen to much, but we only really hear when we let the confusion of voices die, so that only *one* speaks. We look at much, yet we only really see when we have extinguished all the confusing lights, and only the *one* clear light shines in the soul, which is far above all busyness, all fragmentation.

III REPETITION IN MUSIC

Its Significance and Use in Education and Music Teaching

1) Introduction

Repetition is a purely spiritual principle. Like a mathematical law, it is never completely revealed in the world of phenomena. As seldom as two objects can ever be completely identical, so seldom can one experience be exactly the same as another. This difference consequently leaves a space in which a contrasting force, which I would like to call the natural force of 'free opening-up', can commence. Repetition, seen from the point of view of development, is a negative element. Yet, just where outwardly the law of repetition appears in its most exact form, this opposing force often concentrates quite incredibly to form a counter-thrust. And, where this law appears more inwardly, free growth can unfold externally as on firm ground.

The law of repetition applies to the reappearance of a certain event in time. I would also like to speak about repetition when only a part, or component, of an event reappears. The first basic question follows from this: *What* is repeated? It will be shown how varied is the answer given by music. It is not a matter of indifference whether a self-contained event, or one laden with suspense appears twice, or more often. This question must also be put quantitatively, even when the degrees of discrepancy indicate more correspondences.

A further fundamental question is: *When* is the event repeated? Does it immediately follow its initial appearance, does it reappear early; is the repeat heightened through a rest, or even through a contrast? The significance of these subsidiary questions will be revealed in our musical examples.

No less fundamental is the third question: *How often* is an event repeated? In some cases, it will answer itself. Where this question can be put, however, I lay special emphasis upon it.

These three fundamental questions could be placed before each investigation of repetition. I place them intentionally here as general considerations in order to leave open the connection to other areas. Only by answering them are some special points resolved.

I wish to show the musical examples in chronological order in order to illuminate the characteristics of various epochs of musical style, and above all the characteristics of individual composers, too, from a particular standpoint.

2) Repetition in Music and Its Significance

a) Antiquity

In the early stage of its development, music was intimately connected with its sister art, poetry. The elevated speech of Greek drama was song. Dance and movement then appeared as well, so that all three arts which exist in the flow of time were united. The relationships of these arts to one another is not fully understood even today. One thing is clear: 'The text, to which music was sung, had the leading role' (Henry Lang. I. Page 19). So we can assume that the rhythm of the songs essentially followed the metre of the poem. One basic measure, corresponding to the contents, traversed a poem. Its repetition, only interrupted at its conclusion, and the continuous melody circling around a few notes, may have had a tremendous effect on the audience of a Greek drama, or on the priests taking part in an offering service accompanied by music. This effect, however, was of magical compulsion. Certain contents were impressed inexorably upon the consciousness of the audience.

A second sort of repetition is the correspondence of two strophes often employed in the chorus. The concepts: strophe, antistrophe and epodos seem to be of a purely musical terminology. 'Strophe means the self-contained musical phrase as distinct from the "moving hither and thither" of the melody; antistrophe, the corresponding strophe, the opposite piece; and epodos the final or ending song' (Friedrich Schubert. Page 18).

We have here a construction which corresponds to the later song form. In addition to this we already find in the exchange of two semi-choruses between strophe and antistrophe a clarification of what is always expressed when a passage occurs twice. This will be discussed in detail when we consider the music of Bach.

b) The Middle Ages

The four kinds of verse feet [1st metre: trochee (-u), 2nd iambus (u-), 3rd dactylus (-uu), 4th anapaest (uu-)] came into the music of the Middle Ages from the metrical feet of antiquity.

In a Latin Whitsun rondel from Paris (c.1200) (Example 34), the trochaic foot corresponds to the trochaic measure of the text. The rhythmically repeating motif (a) releases spontaneous delight in the listener. A concluding phrase is attached three times to the main part, so that the form — a b a a a b a b — is created. This (b) has the effect that the repeat appears not compulsive but moving freely. (Try as an experiment to sing only (a) five times!) The repetition (that is, sung twice) leaves the listener still free. But after this it must go on further.

From: Adler's *Musikgeschichte*, part 1   Example 34

Often, however, the melodic phrasing is still freely drawn and only the rhythmic framework iş repeated continuously. Yet it contradicts the text, sometimes even departing from it. Thus, in one of the *Cantigas de S. Maria* of Alfons the Wise (thirteenth century) the magical metre (2) in the music conflicts with the trochaic measure of the text. An extract from it makes this plain.

From: Adler's *Musikgeschichte*, part 1   Example 35

The beginning of multiple voices of polyphony brings new phenomena for repetition, too. New principles appear, unconnected with the text. One of the first and most beautiful recorded examples is the canon from England, *Summer is icumen in* (c.1240).

Here the rhythm (metre 1) corresponds with the text. The rapid succession of the four entries effects an overlapping of the textual phrases. Tension appears through the voices pursuing each other closely. As one sinks back, the other usually begins again. Here is an extract:

c. 1240 Example 36

Repetition in the form of imitation also appears in multiple voice settings. A passage from John de Garlandia (early twelfth century) indicates this 'priceless artistic means of imitation' for the first time. It is quoted by Ambros in the following way: 'Music can be coloured through three means: through the ordering of sound (*sono ordinato* ...), through decoration (*florificatione*), and through repetition (*repetitione*). The latter is twofold: either in the same voice (*eiusdem vocis*), when a whole phrase returns in one and the same voice, thus meeting the listener anew as something already known, or in different voices (*repetitio diversae vocis*), when the same phrase (*idem sonus repetitus*) is performed at different times by different voices (*in diverso tempore a divris vocibus*).' With this quotation, a development is actually anticipated, as Ambros remarks. At the same time it expresses an important point of view concerning repetition: something well known meets the listener again. This presupposes, of course, that the listener also recognises it. Whilst the self-repeating metres, as well as the often repeating melody of our rondel were still experienced more in the subconscious, now aural memory of the listener is appealed to. With this, repetition is pushed into the visible realm.

c) The Renaissance

The change of style around 1300 brought new musical forms of expression. The freeing from the art of poetry allowed music to unfold its intrinsic forces. The motet nevertheless retained connecting elements through isorhythms. In the fifteenth and sixteenth centuries, the free melodic phrasing of folk-song often repeats halfway through a stanza (for example, *Innsbruck, ich muss dich lassen*). Metres which remain continuous have completely disappeared. But something else arises: repetition of single melodic notes. Of course they are also to be found in older melodies. Yet there they were present mostly by chance, occurring at unimportant places. Now they assume the task of binding the shifting tonality of a mode. The key-note (Example 37) or the fifth (Example 38) were especially emphasized. Since every note falls on another beat of the bar, repetition does not call up the effect of a chant sung on a monotone. It is much rather contraction, tension, in order to call forth a more free flow of the melody.

Melody c. 1540   Example 37

[musical notation: Der Win—ter ist ver—gan———— gen, ich seh des Mai—— ens Schein]

The song, *Der Morgenstern ist aufgegangen* (Example 38), though written down later, is quite in keeping with this era and shows us, apart from the already-mentioned repetition of the fifth (C), a hidden principle of form: the first four notes of the melody draw together, in seed-like form, the first beat of each of the four lines of the stanza (C, C, A, F, marked X). We have here the phenomenon of a melodic repetition, free in rhythm and time.

Melody c. 1600   Example 38

[Musical notation with lyrics:]
Der Mor-gen-stern ist auf—— ge—gan—gen, er leucht' da—her zu
die—ser Stun——de hoch ü-ber Berg und tie-fe Tal,——
Vor Freud' singt uns die lie——— be Nach——— ti ——— gall.

The contraction of note values, with the note repetition on the third statement (... *hoch über Berg* ...), is an especially strong contraction. It makes it possible for the beginning of each melodic phrase, which up till now has been falling, to change direction. Freely moving, growing strong in inner dynamic through the repeat, the melody halts on the fifth, then to sink down in the longest phrase which spans an octave. With this wonderful example of inner dynamic we recognize clearly the two primal forces of a musical passage, as Mersmann described it.

Inner dynamic, comparable to a force of nature, is held back by a law contradicting it, but is also formed by it.

At this point we should like to investigate the nature of barring. The division into bars, as it is given in Example 38, does not correspond everywhere with the melody. It is superficial and was only added later. With the words *er leucht daher* two 3/4 bars would correspond with the melody. With this we see, as also in regard to the beat, that melodies are often free from the law of repetition. Only in the baroque era was this most hidden element of music also fixed. The constant beat, the continuous repeating metre is the basis of most vocal settings of the ensuing period.

The first forms of purely instrumental music developed in the sixteenth century, starting from song and dance. Dance has its quite special requirements: In it duality prevails, corresponding to the pairing of dancers, and the stepping to right and left. The division of three as *Tripla, Hupfauf* or *Proportz* only appears in the barring and follows a first part which is contained in an even time. The second part of the main dance, standing in contrast to the second part of such a rapid epidance, is shown in Example 39.

Thus we can recognize the simple but characteristic variation of the same element, an example of the retention of the melody while the rhythmic values change. Duality is expressed in the quoted example a a' b. But above all, in the two closing minims we feel ourselves standing on both feet again after the ever-increasing rapid *Springtanz*, leaping dance. The ostinato bass developed from the technique of a bass instrument, for example, bagpipes. Initially, it is but the pillar of the main beat. At the conclusion of the quotation through the accelerated tempo it appears more in the foreground and, agreeing with the basic measure, the self-encircling upper voice flies ever more crazily towards the end. Despite the simple process here, we can feel the importance of the shortened repeat. It is supposed to impose on the dancers a magical compulsion.

From Jacob Paix, *Orgeltabulaturbuch* (1583)   Example 39

d) The Baroque Era

With the beginning of the period of figured bass, the subject of harmony appears in the foreground. Up to now I have left it out, because on the one hand it is simply the result of the free melodic play of all the voices, and on the other hand in it repetition is not to be found in any remarkable way. If, however, we expect in the structure of Protestant hymns, which then stood in the foreground of composition in Germany, an harmonic ossification, then we would be mistaken. While the lower voices adjust completely to the rhythm of the hymn tune, these separate out into an unbelievably manifold and free-flowing harmonic movement. Initially, it follows the inner principle of functional sequence. The cadence appears more strongly as a factor creating tonality. The harmonic appearance, which is so conspicuous in late baroque music, however, is initially to be found only in a suggestive and isolated way.

Thus, the attention is once more directed to the melodic line. A principle of repetition appears now which, later, will assume an important role: the *sequence*. In the Introduction, I have already stated that under the concept of repetition I include the reappearance of single components of a passage. Thus the sequence interests us as repetition of a certain series of intervals. In conventional music theory these two ideas are placed side by side. But because we want to investigate repetition in a comprehensive way, it is possible to subordinate it here.

With the early baroque master, Heinrich Schütz, we can follow how he employs the sequence ever more frequently in the course of his long creative life, and also with increasing clarity in his compositions.

The sequence appears clearly in the 92nd Psalm of the *Becker Psalter* (new version 1661). The harmony follows only occasionally. In the first version, of 1628, this is *still quite free*, and *melodic* sequence is less weighty, through the small deviation and rapid succession of notes (to clarify what has been said, it is enough to quote the melody, and the bass transposed up an octave).

Schütz, 92nd Psalm   Example 40

The many phenomena which are important for us here are developed in a clear sequence. J.S. Bach summarises them in his work. Thus, it seems justified if I now concentrate on him in more detail, hoping to approach the subject, and also Bach's genius, a little more closely.

It would hardly be possible for a commentator on Bach's works to pass by the first Prelude of the *Well-Tempered Clavier*. It is not only a Prelude to a Fugue, it is the Prelude to the whole *Well-Tempered Clavier*. With its wondrous construction it is plainly an archetypal image for the Bach Prelude; at the same time, however, it summarizes what we find repeatedly from early lute music onwards: the plain joy of playing with figuration. The simple, broken chords appear twice in every bar. A magnificent breathing comes into being.

Bach, Prelude in C major (WTC 1)   Example 41

Statement and confirmation, reception and comprehension, these alternate in constant movement. Outwardly, the repeat could not follow more exactly and yet we perceive it coming from the opposite direction. We are reminded of a similar phenomenon in the Psalms: 'Enter into his gates with *thanksgiving*, and into his courts with *praise:* be thankful unto him and *bless* his name!' (Psalms 100, 4). Joh. Gottfried Herder described this parallelism in the following way:

> Both parts strengthen, exalt, confirm each other in their precept or joy. With songs of praise it is obvious: with songs of complaint it is the nature of sighing and lamentation. The taking of a breath consoles and, at the same time, strengthens the soul: the other section of the choir participates in our sorrow and echoes it, or as the Hebrews say, it is the daughter of the voice of our sorrow. With songs of praise, one verse confirms the other: it is as if a father speaks to his son and the mother repeats it. Through this the message becomes true, heartfelt and intimate.

This phenomenon of repetition has hardly ever been put into more beautiful and nobler words. We can transfer them unchanged to the musical sphere. The aspect of poetry shows us at the same time the general validity of the law of repetition.

The beginning of the Prelude quoted (Example 41) shows a self-contained cadence harmonically complete in itself. In bar 5 the sequence follows it. Hans Mersmann described both these form-building methods in the following way:

> The cadence is the self-contained curve from tonic to tonic laying down a basis through which suspense is carried. The sequence has no foundation but changes continuously: we mean by it the reappearance of the same figure, as with a melodic-rhythmic occurrence, as in this instance the same succession functioning on a new level. Cadence is the static, sequence the dynamic principle of harmonic architecture. Cadence corresponds to the enclosed, sequence to the open form. (*Musikhören*. Page 141).

The latter will be discussed in more detail below. The cadence formula in the Prelude appears very often in a similar enclosed way in Bach.

In the *Well-Tempered Clavier*, Part I, 19 of the 24 Preludes begin with the enclosed cadence, fewer do in Part II. The following table summarises them (major keys in capitals, minor keys in small letters):

Enclosed Opening Cadence		Part I	Part II
1)	I, IV, (II), V, I above pedal-point	c, d, E^b, f#, G, g, a	C, D^b
2)	I, IV, V, I with partial pedal-point	C, e^b, E, e, g#	b^b
3)	No pedal-point	D, F	F#
4)	Developed cadence	C#, f, B^b, B	c, E^b
5)	Incomplete cadence I V I	A^b	D, f, f#

I have given special attention to the pedal-point. Bach often begins with it. We can also describe it as one form of repetition. Because of its continual persistence on a fundamental note it is a 'source of strongest harmonic tension and bearer of an often tremendous musical architecture' (Mersmann. Page 57).

Take the opening of the *St Matthew Passion*. Above the tonic E in the bass the whole harmony is developed in unbelievable variety.

A similar effect can be produced by the ostinato bass voice. In the 'Crucifixus' of the *B minor Mass*, it holds the greatest tension in itself. Its ending is the same as the beginning, so that its constant encircling becomes like the image of the Eternal Ground of the World in which everything is contained.

59

Bach, B minor Mass   Example 42

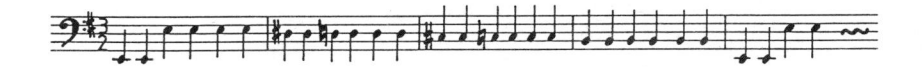

This profoundly based unity appears in two other forms in Bach. The continuo of the *Violin Sonata in F minor* (Example 43) introduces a theme in the first bar. In the second bar the middle voice confirms it, an octave lower. The one-bar theme is repeated eighty-five times in the 108 bars, at different pitches. Only after the violin soars out in melodic movement after sustained notes is it silent, and then, once again unremittingly, it passes through different harmonic degrees. We can say here, that, with this continual changing repetition, two contrasts are combined: unity and multiplicity.

Bach, Violin Sonata in F minor   Example 43

In almost all the pieces by Bach we can find how a movement once begun is continued. In the fugue, repetition of a theme at different registers is the rule. The theme is not developed; it appears at the most in changed form (augmentation, diminution, rhythmical variations, inversion, etc.). Even the instrumentation appearing in the first bars of an aria, for example, from Bach's *St Matthew Passion*, is binding and continues throughout the whole piece. It is the unification of motif, movement and timbre which is so pleasing in Bach's music.

I would like to turn once more to harmony. We have discussed the significance of the cadence formula. In Bach, it appears at the beginning and ending of a movement or a section. In between, however, the harmony moves in sequences. Any attempt to understand this within a functional theory of harmony simply describing individual chords would be very clumsy and would be beside the point. Bach does not often modulate, but moves easily and imperceptibly to ever new levels by fifths. His harmonic structure follows the principle of incessant movement in fifths.

This becomes clear with the *Prelude in C# major* from the *Well-Tempered Clavier*, Book I (Example 44). The first seven bars form an initial cadence (see Table, page 59). In bar 8 the semiquaver movement moves to G# major without modulating, or employing the new leading-note. Here the same cadence pattern is played out with swapped voices on a higher harmonic level. To label this as the dominant would be correct but not essential, for it is not related to the previous part, changing in bars 16 and 24 in exactly the same form as in bar 8, to the next higher fifth level (D# and A# — see Table, page 62).

Bach, C# major Prelude *WTC 1*   Example 44

[musical notation]

Following the four 8-bar cadences described above, where sequences are generally presented, the actual harmonic sequential movement commences. The bass note of each triad moves downwards in three fifths: B#, E#, A#, D#.

Bach, C# major Prelude   Example 45

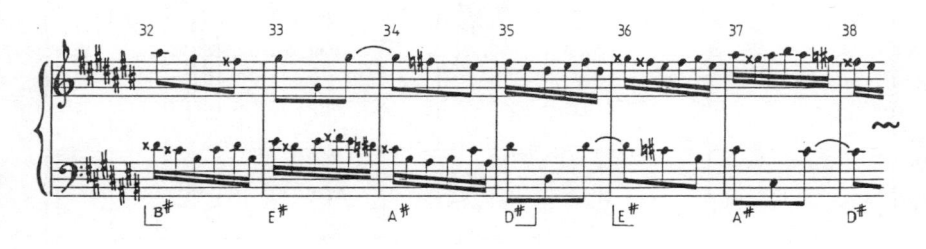

[musical notation]

This is repeated from E# (bar 36), A# and D#. The same appears in whole as in the part: a descent of a fifth through four levels. The correspondence contracted into four bars (Example 45, bar 32-35 = bar 36-39, etc.) penetrates steeply to the tonic level and expands into the first sequence: 8-bar cadence on F# and C# (see Diagram I). On G# (here the dominant, where the great closing cadence is introduced) the frequency condenses again powerfully (2 bars), then expands once again, and (Example 46) passes into a one-bar correspondence.

Bach, C# major Prelude   Example 46

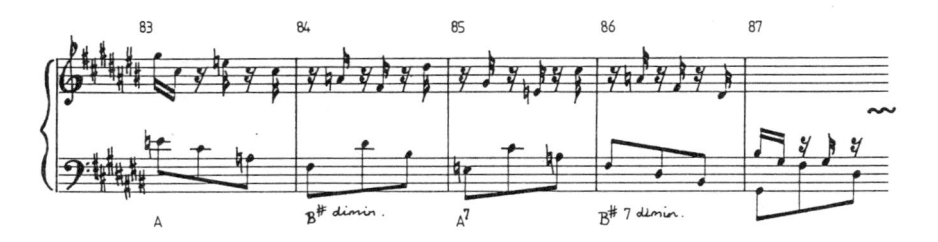

[musical notation: bars 83–87, with chord labels A, B# dimin., A⁷, B# 7 dimin.]

The climax of this *Prelude* is reached: rapid change of the straight sequence (in the form: a b' b' a' here), framing the whole resounding area (G#" to G#) and quick superseding of distant triads (A and B#). The tremendous suspense runs into the broad stream of the final cadence.

Bach, C# major Prelude   Diagram 1

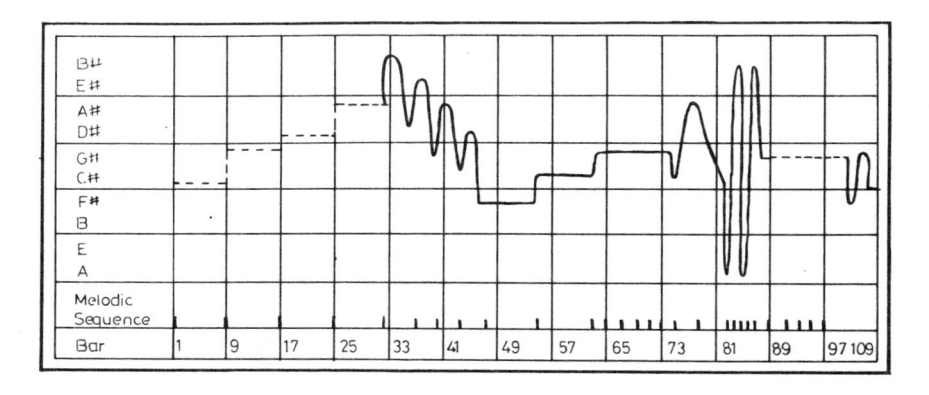

[diagram: harmonic sequence plotted against bar numbers 1, 9, 17, 25, 33, 41, 49, 57, 65, 73, 81, 89, 97 109, with vertical axis levels B#/E#, A#/D#, G#/C#, F#/B, E/A, and a "Melodic Sequence" row]

The opening theme (Example 44) is indicated on the corresponding levels through dashes. The diagram shows clearly how the harmonic sequence moves in great organic curves. Once again, Bach's genius is revealed; the rule is bound to organic growth, the construction takes on life. Bach lets us forget what often leads to mania with the less-gifted composers of the late baroque period. Who would guess that the *Fugue in G minor (Well-Tempered Clavier*

Book II) is subjugated to this law almost without intermission? The theme already contains the descending fifths as framework (Example 47). The inserted third appears later in the harmony, sometimes as bass note of a passing triad. In the melody of the theme the whole harmonic development is concealed.

Bach, Fugue in G minor *WTC II*   Example 47

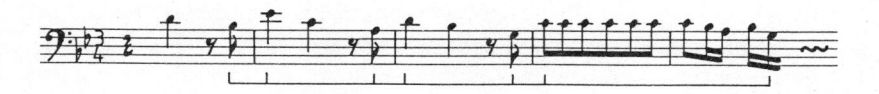

The following analysis of bars 6-17 is to show the almost uninterrupted series of fifths. The triads often change between major (capitals), minor (small letters) and diminished triads (underlined letters). This becomes clear when compared with the three series of seven notes.

g–C   F–B   e– –   ADg   cF–   BE c   a– –   Dgd   g–C

F–B   –e–c   AdG   I (etc.)

A short excerpt from the same Fugue is to show the circle from D minor to D minor (bars 28-32):

Bach, Fugue in G minor   Example 48

d   g   C   F   B♭   g   e   A⁷   d

Whilst the movement in fifths in the *C# major Prelude* is subject to regular agogic, here in the *G minor Fugue* it is not strict in time.

The final example (Example 49) is to show with what conscious skill Bach builds in the series of fifths into the simplest most self-contained form. The 8-bar phase is an inner unity like the scale which is consummated in the octave. In the second Minuet from the first *French Suite*, the series of fifths is combined with this in unsurpassable, classical beauty. The fundamental notes change from D over G, C, F, B^b, E, A and in the final bar re-attain the eighth fifth, the fundamental D with which the piece opens. In bar 9 the circle begins anew (a'). Beginning and ending are the same. A walk through time. Both curves are repeated. The second part (b) announces a contrast (8 bars), in order to re-enter the two circles which come to rest in themselves (a a'::b a a':). The harmony therefore revolves eight times through this wonderful circuit. Here the laws of perfection and beauty, strictness and goodness, calmness and unfolding are at one with each other.

Bach, Menuet II from 1st French Suite   Example 49

This continuously repeating circling of fifths, the incessant movement discussed above, and the rising from the pedal-point which contains everything within itself, are, with Bach, the image of something grander. Goethe expresses this:

Wenn im Unendlichen dasselbe
Sich widerholend ewig fliesst
Das tausendfältige Gewölbe
Sich kräftig ineinander schliesst;
Strömt Lebenslust aus allen Dingen,
Dem kleinsten wie dem grössten Stern,
Und alles Drängen, alles Ringen
Ist ewige Ruh' in Gott dem Herrn.

When in the infinite the same pattern
Repeats itself in eternal flux,
And the thousandfold vault of heaven
Mutually supports itself,
Then joy of life streams from all things,
From the smallest to the greatest of stars,
And all yearning, all struggle
Is eternal rest in God the Lord.

e) Classicism

We stand at the beginning of a new period of musical style, though in the compositions we still find elements initially from the previous age. 'Mozart who, like Bach, turns back, summing up all the strengths of his century' (Mersmann. Page 147), exhibits phenomena which remind us immediately of Bach. The descending fifth is hardly to be found in Beethoven any more. With Mozart, it appears in the earlier as well as the later works. In the first instance it is limited only to the lightweight transitions, whilst the themes point to the future, calling on the spirit of development. An example taken from the *Piano Sonata* (K. 545):

Mozart, Piano Sonata (K. 545)   Example 50

The minor section included in the last movement of the late F *major Sonata* (K. 533) possesses a polyphonic character (Example 51). It moves in wonderful steps of a fifth. Does not the contemplative nature of this section recall music of the baroque age?

Mozart, Piano Sonata in F major (K. 533)   Example 51

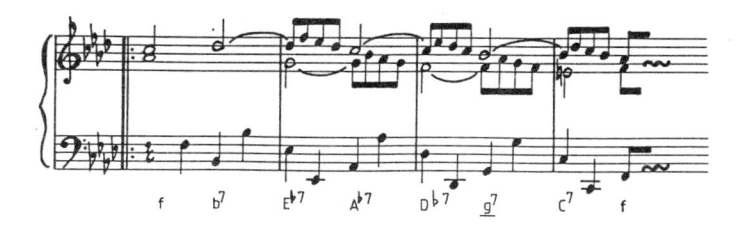

In Mozart's last work, the *Requiem*, the principle of repetition combines with the thematic material. In this conscious application we recognize a singular occurrence in musical history: a master approaching the completion of his life, makes himself once more a pupil at the feet of a master. Mozart, three years before his death, studied the works of Bach.

Mozart, from Domine Jesu, *Requiem*   Example 52

Let us turn to another side of Mozart. His sensitive reticence and amiable playfulness are expressed in the many repetitions of short notes and accented passing notes. They form suspense on a small scale. But they also appeal to our consciousness. The intense movement of the upward leap of a third in the Rondo of the above-mentioned *Sonata in F major* does not sink back into diatonic uniformity (Example 53). It is retained by the harmonic change in the next bar. Through this, its natural force of movement is held back. Our attention is awakened — but in the next moment the tension is relinquished in light quavers. The melody springs back step by step to the tonic and — as though he wanted to say: 'Do you not believe me yet?' — Mozart repeats this roguish epilogue for confirmation, before he moves on.

Mozart, F major Piano Sonata   Example 53

We find this mood of sensitive reticence created through accented passing notes in all classical rondos. Beethoven also reveals the amiable side to his nature here. The last movement from the E^b *Sonata* op. 7 holds back the descending diatonic of the upbeats in the first two bars through accented passing notes (Example 54). These small constrictions give rise to a broad flowing movement in the music.

Beethoven, Rondo from Sonata op. 7 — Example 54

Another example of note repetition in this Rondo theme runs through the lower voice: the continuous falling back of the reappearing dominant note. It sounds throughout, lending tonal security to the uncomplicated theme (Example 54). Because this note is always interrupted on the main beat, its repetition does not appear oppressive, as is somewhat the case in the middle section of Chopin's 'Raindrop' Prelude.

At this point I would like to turn once more to repetition in greater extended forms. I already drew up the formal scheme with the Whitsun rondel from the twelfth century (Example 34). Guido Adler, who republishes it, notes: 'in performance, the chorus (refrain) and soloists (the remaining part) could alternate' (Page 184). This rondel was also sung to secular (profane) French texts. At that time it was the social gathering which breaks out into the refrain, listening again, in the parts between, to the solo singer in their midst. The familiar round was an exchange of doing and listening. Does it not occur in a similar way when listening to a Beethoven rondo?

We open up completely in the uncomplicated main theme. We stand back from it in the inserted middle section in order to join in once more upon its return. Here a great breath is created, which we experience as health-giving. The phrase, 'repetition constricts development', is not applicable here. This form, both on a large scale (ABA) or small (aaba), is an enclosure and not development. Here repetition becomes a positive element.

Now we still have to show how subtly Mozart uses repetition to trigger off *development*.

The second subject of the *G major String Quartet* (K. 387), which begins lightly, is held fast with three chords. On the third chord the melody seeks to free itself through the shaking semiquavers and, meeting the upbeat, it jumps away to the fifth. The lower voices are released in a broad flow. Once again the melody unites with the general sonority, to spread out then in still larger curves. Concentration and release confront each other. Here what is repeated is not the encircling movement, as in Bach, nor an enclosed form like a rondo. All the elements are repeated, following each other immediately in order to form a curve over the small phrase form.

Mozart, String Quartet in G major (K. 387)   Example 55

With this, one effect of repetition is indicated which Beethoven uses in manifold ways and on every scale, thus damming up the development. In the *beginning* the urging force is strengthened, at the *end* it is reined in again through repetition. The number of repeats is important here. With Bach, the single repeat was discussed. It appeared as a breath of confirmation. We can easily imagine that for Beethoven's developed movements this is no longer enough. He does employ it, yet mostly coupled with the double repeat (for example, 2 x 3 or 3 x 2). By means of this he attains the basis for development.

Just as little as we can pass over Bach's *C major Prelude*, discussed above, so it is impossible to ignore Beethoven's first *Piano Sonata*. In the theme (called an evolution theme by Mersmann) the start of the development is hidden by the threefold start (Example 56). The sequence of the first bars could rise in a second repetition to the note C. Beethoven holds back the development in that he lets the path of the highest notes (A^b, B^b) run back once more, and only then achieves the goal (C).

Beethoven, Piano Sonata op. 2/1   Example 56

The two-bar theme is already laden with tension. Through the principle of repetition, which enters the melodic passage in the form of sequences here, it concentrates together for a development of some strength. The accumulation of sequences in the eight bars can be represented thus:

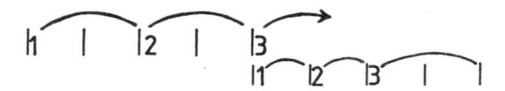

The second entry of the theme is limited to a single ascent. The voices take over the ending triplets of the theme in a balanced exchange (Example 57). This duality results in calmness and breath!

Beethoven, op. 2/1   Example 57

The second subject again releases development through its threefold beginning (Example 58). If we try to proceed to the upward striving quaver movement *without* the second repeat, we find it impossible. The third entry, however, calls for complete development.

Beethoven, op. 2/1   Example 58

Even the coda is still development. It intensifies by the second repeat to a strong broadened *ff* ending, which receives the mighty development of the whole exposition.

Beethoven, op. 2/1   Example 59

The first subject of op. 2/3 and of the *First Symphony* are formed in a similar way to the first subject of this sonata.

The theme of the B^b *major Sonata* op. 22 begins three times in exactly the same way. This strong holding back immediately results in such a broad development that a further reference to the main theme is no longer necessary.

Beethoven, Piano Sonata op. 22   Example 60

Let us turn to other themes. The opening of the last movement of the Sonata op. 10/1 follows exact repetition and soars ever higher through this.

Beethoven, Piano Sonata op. 10/1   Example 61

In this regard we recall the *E minor Sonata* of Haydn. There, the persistent E minor triad causes the development to flow.

Haydn, Piano Sonata in E minor   Example 62

The movement discussed up till now, whose main themes always flow into their development through the threefold beginning, I should like to summarize as the first type of sonata movement.

We can recognize a second type in the E^b *Sonata*, op. 7. In its first subject it appears well-balanced through the single repeat, resting in itself. Only the pounding quavers urge forwards.

Beethoven, Piano Sonata op. 7   Example 63

Only in the next phrase does the development commence through a threefold beginning (Example 64). With this steeply ascending sequence we ask ourselves: What is the driving force? The simple movement of the lower voice played by itself appears meaningless in the sequence. The upper voice circling around itself and the calming middle voice are not the answer either. In the simultaneous, contradictory forces (repetition and growth) we recognize the tremendous force of tension.

Beethoven, op. 7   Example 64

In bar 25 the opening theme appears once again in *ff*. Now it is repeated *twice* and is opened up for development.

The theme of op. 10/1 follows the same principle of construction. Here, too, the single repetition is not sufficient to produce a greater development. A second beginning is necessary, which through its triple nature draws forth the flow of secondary phrases.

Now let us choose a theme which retains its soaring twofold character also in its second beginning. In op. 31/3 Beethoven is drawn by necessity to begin for a third time. Only this third beginning, which appears in the minor, moves over into the flowing countertheme.

Beethoven: op. 31/3   Example 65

I hope that these examples have shown clearly how important repetition becomes for musical development. The effect of the threefold beginning is also clear. Its significance from the musical point of view will be briefly discussed here. (I will go into it in more detail in section IV.) Classicism frequently constructed its melodies in the externally symmetrical and simplest form, the sentence. The four- or eight-bar phrase controls it. The threefold beginning of a motif — be it one, two or more bars — never completely takes this time. Thus the form, despite its external symmetry, remains inwardly open and stretches out beyond its confined framework. How differently the quadruple law works, filling space, will be discussed with op. 7 (Example 69).

Repetition for the development of sonata form is an essential principle on a large scale too. As the repetition of a motif does not lessen its development but intensifies it, so does the repetition of the exposition of the sonata. Mersmann holds that this repetition, following an old account, is only justified

> so long as the first part is limited to presenting themes or similar things. When, however (as in Beethoven's *First Symphony* which he discusses), development already occurs within the exposition, whose unique character appears just as unrepeatable as the first Act of a drama, then we may also dispense with the composer's directions (Page 161).

From the foregoing discussion, this conclusion appears questionable to me. In the recommencement of the exposition especially, I see a strengthening of the force of development, which then, in the third beginning, the recapitulation, so gains in strength that it can lead over to the new: to the further movements of the sonata or symphony, whose inner connection with the first movement Mersmann demonstrates so excellently. Can we ignore the threefold element here?

Let us take from Beethoven's *second movements* one which is relevant to our subject.

The Allegretto from the *Seventh Symphony* takes up an old architectural principle of construction. The regular rhythm in its strictly measured pace recalls a Greek chorus. The harmony is expressed in clear homophonic chords. The melody is initially bound to the upper voice which is repeated. The theme stands before us in three 8-bar phrases (a b b). Then there begins an arrangement of this somewhat rigid theme which reappears twelve times in inexorable strictness.

Beethoven, Symphony No. 7 — Example 66

In addition, the ending is somewhat strange here. The fascinating, seemingly endless rhythms are suddenly blocked off (after the homophony of the whole movement) through polyphonic entries following each other ever more rapidly. The *forte* intensifies the effect. Beethoven had to free himself energetically from the compulsion of these rhythms.

Beethoven, Symphony No. 7 — Example 67

The *third movement* of the Haydn symphony received a reshaping by Beethoven. The simple minuet gave way to the scherzo. The minuet was a dance. Like the theme of Example 6 from the pre-baroque era, it was based on duality. A section from the Minuet of the Sonata op. 2/1 will serve to make this clear.

Beethoven, op. 2/1   Example 68

The scherzo no longer has anything to do with dance. Only the form (a b a) and the time signature correspond to the minuet. Beethoven's forming power intrudes into this movement: the triple element, the tendency to development — contradicting the old dance — gives it a new character and, above all, builds it into the symphony or sonata as a complete entity. (Consider the complete fusion in the fourth movement of the *Fifth Symphony*.)

To conclude our observations regarding Beethoven, I would like to show how and when he employs a more frequent repetition. We recognized the double repeat as the *starting point* for development. The *triple* repetition is then introduced — corresponding to its character — when a development is *completed*. It gives the listener the feeling of security, satisfaction or triumph. The above-mentioned *Sonata* op. 7, whose theme only slowly began to enter into development, reaches a satisfying completion only after the second subject has been heard.

Beethoven, op. 7   Example 69

Now to *more frequent repetition*. The last movement of the *E major Sonata* op. 14/1, begins with a splendid rising melody in the upper voice. The accompaniment flows downwards in broken triads. While these flow on continuously, the melody stays suddenly quiet on the fourth degree of the scale and is repeated six times. This does not bear any relationship to the initial development. It is stuck, and finally comes to a standstill on the chord of the dominant seventh.

Beethoven, op. 14/1   Example 70

In the theme of the *Sixth Symphony* no development occurs in the sense so far discussed. The breakthrough to the dominant at the end of the first thematic curve, is repeated once, twice — here it could be confirmation — thrice, four times and even further. 'Here nothing more grows; beginning or aim is hardly present, but there is only a moving and circling without growth or purpose' (Mersmann. Page 155).

Beethoven, Symphony No. 6   Example 71

Forces are expressed here which, in their inexhaustible primeval nature, the European admires and fears in the people of the Far East. They live in the ecstatic songs of joy as well as in melancholic songs of lament (Example 72). The endlessness of *space* speaks through them. Time retreats. The same thing is repeated without an end, that is, it is irrelevant whether something returns five times or ten times. To make this clear, two Russion folksongs are inserted here. In the first, it is the happy opening with which each of the eight lines of this short love song begins. In the second, it is the lamenting, melancholy ending into which the twelve half-lines of every verse of this sad song flow. (The numbers give the order of the repeated lines.)

from *Das Lied der Völker*   Example 72

[musical notation]
1,2| 5,6| 9,10   3,4|7,8|11,12
1/3/5   2/4/6

If these forces are explained through Beethoven in the form of wild high spirits, how often do we find examples in fine art music too, where they sink down in melancholic monotony! Mozart uses them, too. How strange is the effect of the monotonous minor section in the light series of variations from the first *Piano Trio in G major* (K. 496), that monotonous motif of the violin above the unremitting movement of fourths in the cello.

Mozart: Piana Trio in G major (K. 496)   Example 73

[musical notation]

Melancholy in Mozart! Today we have outgrown the habit of speaking of the 'ever cheerful Mozart'. Here, however, a special side of Mozart is revealed. Is it deep loneliness, is it longing or an intimation of infinity? I would like to leave that to the individual listener. It is surely one of the most revealing, strangest passages in Mozart's work.

The connection of this apparently endless repetition with the capabilities and forces of Eastern peoples is expressed in a poem by Goethe from the *Buch des Hafis* (West-östlicher Divan), the first verse of which is quoted:

Dass du nich enden kannst, das macht dich gross,
Und dass du nie begingst, das ist dein Los.
Dein Lied ist drehend wie das Sterngewölbe
Anfang und Ende immerfort dasselbe
Und was die Mitte bringt, ist offenbar
Das, was zu Ende bleibt und Anfangs war.

That you cannot end, makes you great,
That you can never begin, that is your fate.
Your song revolves like the starry vault
Beginning and ending continually the same
And what the middle brings is obviously
What remains at the end and was there from the beginning.

(Mersmann likewise quotes the opening of this verse in connection with Beethoven's *Sixth Symphony*, but without referring to the special eastern character it possesses.)

f) Romanticism

After a discussion of Beethoven's works, to turn to Romanticism is almost like back-pedalling. For, in many respects, the Romantics are like imitators compared with this great master whose work points far into the future. We feel this most strongly at the turning point. When I therefore discuss Schubert first, I do so more to approach his personality, and, at the same time, to discuss many phenomena which remained untouched in the previous chapter.

The repetition of short notes which I discussed with Mozart appears very often with Schubert, too. In those Mozart examples, their charm, combined with a light emphasis on a note (I called it a 'becoming-conscious'), becomes an accented passing-note with the change of harmony. With Schubert, this way of expression becomes still more reticent. The repetition of notes is often embedded in repeated triads, and especially in simple accompaniment figures as minimum tension — it develops flow and movement. Schubert's nature is expressed in this subtle holding back and letting go.

Schubert, Sonata op. 120   Example 74

A similar phenomenon is mirrored in the symmetrical form of several of his melodies. The theme of the *Unfinished Symphony* shows us clearly how far removed he is from the drama of Beethoven. His inner symmetry contradicts the evolution, which with Beethoven we can recognize in the second subjects of most of his sonata movements.

Schubert, B minor Symphony   Example 75

In his instrumental works, the master of Lied cannot keep silent. Everything becomes song with Schubert. His symphonic creations bear witness to his great gift, but also to his tragedy. He preferred the short form and its modifications to the development form. From the beginning, certain principles of repetition inherent in song are given in the text. The rhyme of two lines calls forth its correspondence in the music. Certainly, the beginning of the song in Example 37 is repeated with the corresponding line of the text. Schubert, however, often surmounts the formulation bound to the text. A formal picture evolves from the first song from *Die schöne Müllerin* (Example 76), reminding us almost of a Bach Prelude: cadence − sequence − cadence. Here it is: repetition − sequence − repetition. The 'picture' arising for the listener is bound to the textual content: the self-enclosed statement *'Das Wandern ist des Müllers Lust, das Wandern!'* ('The miller's desire is to wander, to wander!') is repeated like an echo, and, intensified through the uniformity in the accompaniment, recalling the encircling thoughts which the wanderer cherishes and to which the environment seemingly summons him again like an echo. Then he starts up from his musing *'Das muss ein schlechter Müller sein, dem niemals fiel das Wandern ein ...'* ('It must be a bad miller who has never had the desire to wander ...') to sink back again into the old dreaming, which is confirmed by the echo.

Schubert, 'Das Wandern' from *Die Schöne Müllerin*　　　　　　Example 76

The song is strophic. What I pointed out in the first verse does not depend upon a special text and is consequently applicable to all the verses.

Schubert, however, often seeks to lend expression to the new thought of a verse through variations. In doing so, repetition is restricted. As in the art of poetry, where the form remains constant, in music it is certain elements, almost always that of form. I would like here to mention the general whole realm of variations. (That I only touch on these in this work is justified by the main aim. I do not wish to look at well-known and much discussed forms, but − as has become clear in the meantime − try to show the effect of a certain phenomenon with examples.)

In Schubert's *D minor Quartet*, the series of variations starts as if for a great development. The theme is rhythmically 'metrical', constructed like the theme from Beethoven's *Seventh Symphony*, discussed above (Example 66). Its intensity is lent to it by the song from which it is taken *(Death and the Maiden)*. The homophonic setting strengthens the effect of the rhythms through the 'simultaneous repetition'.

In Variation I, the rhythms appear mostly in the cello, in a muffled *pizzicato*. In Variation II on the cello they flow into a free line, but on the viola they are concentrated in a diminution so that they experience the greatest condensation in Variation III. Pressed together in the smallest space, played by all instruments *ff*, the rhythms show the greatest tension through their static pounding. Yet already in the next variation the force of the rhythms dissolves into a broad line. The mood is brightened up by the change to the major. At the end of the last variation, standing in the minor, Schubert reaches the final solution in the major. In discussing the song, Mersmann no longer calls this change repetition. Especially with regard to variation form, I must, however, once more recall my fundamental principle that the reappearance of previous sections should also be discussed in terms of repeats. Variations often reach a complete transformation of values and yet something always remains — visibly or hidden — which, from a new viewpoint, only appears in a fresh light.

Schubert, String Quartet in D minor.   Example 77

We find such a reinterpretation of values in other places of romantic works too. With the favourite jump at that time into the mediant key, the shared mediant note is often repeated and seems to be something completely new as if raised on to a transcendent level. An example from Bruckner's *Fourth Symphony* should clarify this. The first theme ends on a F major triad. The root is carried on in the horns and with the entry of the second subject it becomes the third of D^b major:

Bruckner, Symphony No. 4   Example 78

The musical means of expression of Romanticism rest almost throughout on Classicism. Thus the chord of the diminished seventh already received a special emphasis in Beethoven as a chord of suspense. With Weber and the later Romantics, however, it becomes a constant means of expression for a demonic element. This effect comes from the fact that all the intervals are equidistant. Repetition of this interval has a magical effect. Playing other intervals of the same size in adjacent series has a similar effect (for example, in the chromatic or in the whole-tone scales, as used by the Impressionists).

This harking back to the baroque age is expressed in different ways in Romanticism. It is interesting for us that the descending fifth appears again. Brahms employs it at the beginning of op. 117/2 in its pure form, as Bach did, but he intensifies it with the second beginning as a chain of dominant seventh chords. A short extract from both series is given below.

Brahms, Intermezzo op. 117/2   Example 79

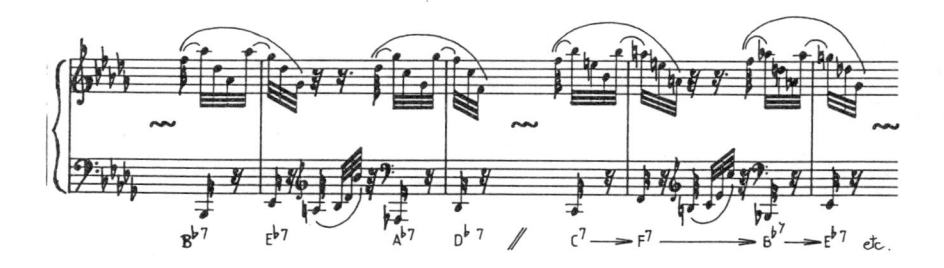

The correspondence with the baroque age becomes especially clear with Bruckner. (I am quite aware that from the stadpoint of today we view, and have to view, the baroque and romantic ages as widely separated. Nevertheless parallels are present which should not be overlooked.) For Bruckner, as for Bach, resting on the keynote is the starting point of vast developments. They rise in 'symphonic waves' (Ernst Kurth) and sink back again to their initial state. A circle is completed here, as with Bach.

Apart from the pedal-point and the clearly stated cadence as starting point of development, it is the repeat that occurs once, affirming everything, which recalls Bach. This becomes clear at the end of the great gesture in Bruckner's *Fourth Symphony* (see Example 78). But in the beginning, too, where Beethoven requires the *threefold element* as a spur to development, with Bruckner there stands a breathing *dual element*.

g) Modern Times

It would be easy to show in recent music many of the forms of repetition discussed above. Here we shall limit ourselves to the most important ones.

The bond with major/minor tonality, lasting roughly two hundred years, led, in Romanticism, to ever more complicated exploitations of harmonic means. With Wagner's *Tristan and Isolde* a breakthrough to new possibilities was accomplished. The danger of what is called 'atonality', however, often could not be circumvented. Only decades later were new musical means of expression established. However, they were more formed and more individual than those of the previous age. Now the new, unusual forms of tonality had to be made credible to the listener, and repetition was a chief means in achieving this.

In Bartok's *Subject and Reflection* (*Microcosmos* No. 141, Book 6) five notes of a minor scale are mirrored exactly. Reflection is a purely spiritual principle related to repetition. To place an 'undertone' series against the overtone series has been frequently attempted. It was not possible to establish this physically. It always remained a transcendent principle. To secure this reflection, Bartok limits himself in the first section to the following seven notes (E^b F G^b A^b ♮B^b ♮ D E^b F). In the second section he builds up the same scale starting from B^b, ascending and descending. Then further from D, E^b F#, G and again from B^b. The beginning (from B^b) and the third section (from D) are given below:

Bartock, *Microcosmos* No. 141   Example 80

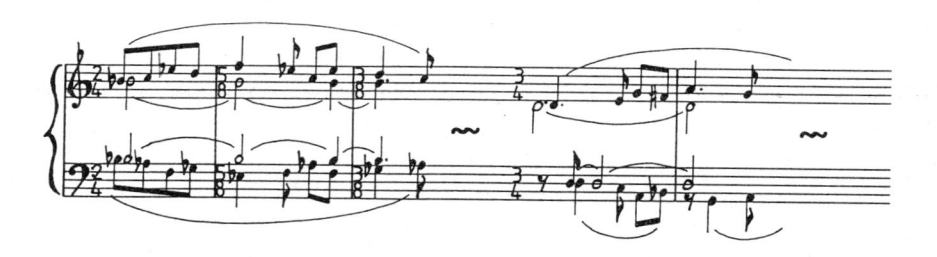

Thus not only the structure of the reflection scale accords with the principle, but also the row of intermediate notes, each time ascending by a minor second and a minor third alternately (B^b, B, D, E^b, F#, G, B^b), until the starting note is reached again and the circle is closed once more.

Bartok, *Microcosmos* No. 141 — Diagram 2

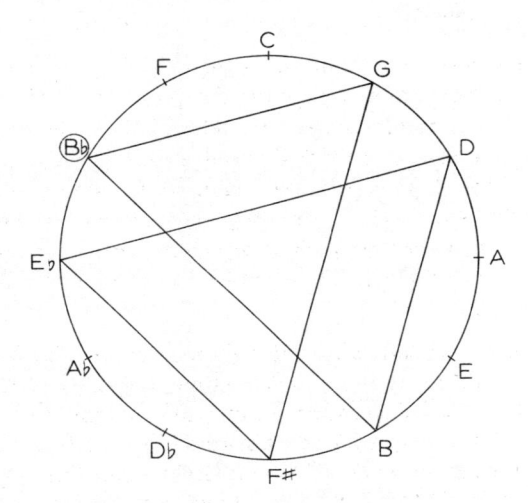

Involuntarily, we recall the falling fifths of Bach; this takes place within the compass of the seven notes of the scale, whilst Bartok goes round the whole circle of fifths (see Diagram 2). At the same time, this complete symmetry of repetition recalls the diminished seventh chord of Romanticism, discussed above. This, however, was apparent by its effect, whilst the principle here carries the free unfolding of melody, and the listener is not aware of it.

The kinship to Bach, which many contemporary composers frequently strive after, appears with Bartok in many of his works in downright astonishing clarity. We already saw above how strictly he follows the principles upon which his work is based. Free organic growth develops on this basis, without our noticing how we are bound to it. This natural uniting of opposing principles makes us admire Bartok as a master. He gives us a monument to his connection with Bach in the piece, *Hommage à J. S. B.* (*Microcosmos* No. 79, Book III). Starting from the simple cadence, the 'Bach-like' figuration moves through eight bars in constant motion (in Example 81 written out as chords to the eighth bar). In bar 9 a contraction of the repetition begins, almost unnoticed by the listener, is condensed even more, circles around itself in a chromatic sequence (bar 11 and 12) and is released again in an oscillating play at a distance of one beat, in order that the major and minor triads may appear facing each other and play around each other in closest proximity at the ending. Not only the figuration reminds us of Bach but especially the narrowing and broadening of oscillation in the whole construction. (Think of the C# major Prelude — Example 46.)

Bartok, *Microcosmos* No. 79   Example 81

Up to now I have barely mentioned the limits of repetition. From an opposite viewpoint we could extensively pursue such a theme as 'Organic Growth in Music'. Mersmann arrives thus at far-reaching limitations of repetition in the oft-quoted book, *Musikhören*. With Bach, however, we saw how repetition rightly employed can extend tremendously far (for example, in the fundamental-note series of fifths, or in the perpetual motion running throughout a movement). Its possibilites in other places are strictly limited. I mentioned repetition of the same intervals (for example, the minor second in chromatic writing, the minor third in the chord of the diminished seventh, etc.), and attempted to show that with more frequent repetitions, the natural force of growth always dies, and the rule appears as a rigid and lifeless image. This use of repetition is intentional and can lead us to the borders of what is reasonable. Hindemith inserts a rushing headlong middle section into the *Sehr lebhaften* (very lively) second movement of his *Third Piano Sonata* (1936) (Example 82). The upper voice rushes about accumulating a series of major and minor thirds senselessly. The border of reasonable repetition is overstepped here. Feverish beating chords are repeated in the ostinato accompaniment. Here the demons of a throbbing machine are craving expression.

Hindemith, Piano Sonata No. 3 — Example 82

To conclude the musical considerations, I should like to mention once again the primal contrast of natural growth and spiritual law. We can observe it everywhere. The masters were able to surmount it in the most differing ways. I tried to show in both examples from Bartok how strongly both principles oppose each other and at the same time unite. It does not originate only with the creativity of individual composers! Today the composer is hindered in a special way with the endeavours of two contrary tendencies, 'neo-tonal' techniques and 'twelve-note' techniques. The former proceeds from the natural force of growth, the latter from the spiritual principle of the twelve-note row. Certainly 'neo-tonal' music will have to subject itself repeatedly to spiritual principles. Opposing this, music pre-supposing the principle of ever-repeating twelve-note rows will demand growth and diversity to the highest degree in its further evolving. I would prefer not to judge here how far this has already been achieved. In any case music could also come about here, combining the opposites of spirit and nature, principle and growth, unity and variety.

IV THE USE OF REPETITION IN TEACHING AND EDUCATION

1) Introduction

'Repetition is a purely spiritual principle. Like a mathematical law, it is never completely revealed in the world of sense experience ...' With these words, I prefaced the previous section. The question should now be appended: Through what means, however, is the law made manifest?

The human mind is able to apprehend and describe laws. The mind discovers in the trajectories of projectiles the physical law of the parabola. It discovers laws of growth in organic nature. In his *'The Metamorphosis of Plants'*, Goethe shows how the unfolding of the plant is based on a constant law.

Yet Goethe repeatedly points from science to another area of human spiritual striving: 'He, to whom Nature begins to reveal her open secrets, feels an irresistible longing for her most worthy expounder, Art' (from *'Maxims and Reflections'*). And, even more clearly, Goethe expresses the task of art ('beauty') when he says: 'Beauty is a manifestation of secret laws of nature, which, without its appearance, would remain eternally hidden from us' (ibid.).

Through the human being, laws of nature become manifest. Through his activity they are formed anew. Then, moreover, they form him, for they are there *through* him and *for* him. The significance of art for pedagogy, as for human education in general, is recognized by everyone, for through it a higher ideal than mere utility manifests to us. Art is the work of great masters. It speaks for itself. That we nevertheless discuss one of its laws is also justified through Goethe's words: 'Art is the mediator of the inexpressible; therefore it appears foolish to want to convey it again through words. Yet, in that we strive to do it, the understanding is so much enriched that the practising capacity also benefits.'

The practice of artistic ability is not merely the business of the artist. Everybody, albeit in a humble measure, can accomplish something in the realm of art. Is not life itself an art? 'Verily, to become human is an art,' said Novalis. Through our own doing we recognize a work of art. Let us now turn in this direction. This section will explore the development of the growing human being and its relationship to that of humanity as a whole. Although the relationship can be demonstrated through many musical examples and through other historical sources, here it will only be indicated through the plan of the whole essay, without being fully substantiated. Nevertheless, the plan is justified; clear evidence of this relationship does exist.

2) Imitation

If the question is asked: How does a child acquire a connection to music before his sixth or seventh year? I would answer: Children need to acquire no connection at all, for an already inherent connection is quite evident, if our concept of music is broad enough. The small child lives completely in his environment of sound, completely in his senses. We need only ask: How does he break away from this being-at-one with all its phenomena?

How often do adults fail to understand the fact that the child spontaneously imitates everything it experiences. A loving word from its mother, father putting his foot down, everything is straightaway faithfully copied by the child. A moral sermon is often received light-heartedly, for the child does not understand the moralistic content, and the pathetic-sounding words call up its readiness to imitate! This usually annoys the 'big people' of course, as St. Exupéry so poignantly characterises them in *The Little Prince*. In the world everything good, but also everything bad, is there to be imitated. What a lofty demand for the educator! He must observe his own 'musical' being, that is, what is heard by the children. Education can only be achieved through good example. And the more musical the educator's words are, the more easily they are accepted by them. Children perceive the rhythm of speech. Inherently musical language has an especially strong effect. Poems, rhythmically scanning phrases and verses; the one-year-old child already listens to them and is delighted. You can repeat them uncountable times throughout the day; children love them and cannot hear them often enough. It is the same inclination with the eastern races, as I tried to show through the examples of the Russian folk-songs, for they, like small children, have not got such a strong connection to time. They are nearer eternity: 'Heaven still remains open for children,' says the proverb.

Soon children try not only to imitate what they hear; they want to set everything into movement. The connection of word, music and movement is evident. This stage reminds us of Greek music.

Melody gradually joins the child's sense of rhythm. Beginning with the falling third, it expands to the pentatonic and binds itself to repetitive rhythms. The feeling for tonality is far removed from the young child. The pentatonic mood with its simple sequence without a keynote, moving and flowing freely, corresponds to the child's nature. Children are at home everywhere, receiving everything, and feeling at one with everything. They are themselves a copy of their environment.

3) Breath and Consciousness

Its awakening consciousness increasingly separates the child from the world. Through this, it faces the world with ever greater wakefulness. However, the fullness of impressions, which it wants to absorb, initially disturbs the child's natural organization. Its breathing is affected particularly strongly. More than ever is this the case in this technical age. Think of the multiplicity of impressions which rush past city children on their way to school. Is it surprising that, in singing, breathlessness appears to such a frightening extent today? Breathlessness can be noticed in all subjects but most obviously in music. But by means of music it must be healed again. A rhythmical regularity should run through the lessons. Breath in a constant pulse, breath in the repeat. Whereas small children will spontaneously sing any tune they hear, when growing out of the stage of imitation they will learn to listen more consciously. Thus the singing teacher can practise rounds with the class. Not only do they stimulate suspense and mutual attention in the children, they become again an expression of a great breathing. Repetition is projected into space and time. Think of the Whitsun rondel or of other forms of rounds as they can be found in folk-song. Think also of the dual element we discussed with Bach.

When we look through the school music of Karl Orff, we find in the first melodies the continuous circling of repeats, as it corresponds to the young child. Then, however, the dual element stands in the foreground.

Orff, *Schulwerk* I, page 14   Example 83

Orff uses the pentatonic scale for all his melodies but nevertheless they often tend towards a tonal centre, as in our example. The ending on C, through the emphasis of the fifth, no longer floats, as would be appropriate for pure pentatonic and for the small child. Through this fact a more natural transition is created to the songs of primary school age. The keynote, arrived at here from above, becomes established through repetition. It impresses itself upon the children's more awakened consciousness. It can make links with the help of aural memory. Children around nine years old recognize the same notes in the melody with delight. These become props for recognition in singing and for making music during lessons. From these notes melodies can unfold more freely and can loosen themselves from the metrical rhythms of earlier children's songs.

A further step is the recognition of repeated phrases in a melody or, later, in a movement (minuet, rondo, etc.). The literal repetition, and, as an extension, the sequence, place minimal demands on the perceptive abilities of the pupils. Through these observations, active listening becomes trained through songs or small pieces of music. A further way is paved at the end of which stands understanding of longer musical works. These techniques, as Riemann stresses, are also useful to amateurs. It is only

> practice and goodwill that are necessary to gain an understanding of long and complicated musical works of art. If a whole work is not to disintegrate into an orderless jumble of single impressions, each having only minimal intensity, then one part should support, lift and intensify the other (be it through analogy or through contrast). Thus it is not only necessary to take in separate parts but also consciously to follow the entire context, that is, to possess a good *ability to memorize* and a *mental ability to synthesize*. In other words, when we come to listen to higher artistic, musical forms, then the possibility of appreciating music only passively ceases. A mere submission to impressions, however willing, must come to an end. It now becomes essential to *make an effort to become involved* (Musik-Ästhetik. Pages 43-4).

The mental ability to synthesize, of which Riemann speaks, is also a prerequisite for education. Only when this awakens in a child can formal education begin. The separation from the world which occurs with awakening consciousness is bridged through this mental ability. The ability only develops, however, through the power of memory. This enables images to be retained, so that their reappearance can be recognized. Memory is strengthened through repetition. Consequently, each lesson builds on repetition of the subject matter. The exercising of mental capacities implies repetition, as does practice of a piece of music, and what I have still to point out regarding the latter will be related to the former.

In both cases it is especially important that a day, or better a night, lies between what is learned and its repetition. Every practising musician knows that what he tries in vain to teach his fingers one day, works much better the following day. During sleep, when consciousness is extinguished, the capacity to memorize appears to be renewed and can link up with what has been received. It is one of the enigmatic 'nadirs' which intervene between all phases of life and of growth. The day's rhythms, which I would like to discuss in the last section, turn into one great breath.

Experience of teaching, especially in the lower classes, shows that often only very little of what was taught even in a single lesson is remembered by the pupil. Regular repetition, which follows the great breath rhythms, alone achieves progress. This becomes very important in music lessons which recur after longer intervals of time, especially in the upper school.

From art, the teacher can learn how to apply repetition, and indeed everything to do with teaching and education. The theme of a sonata or a rondo, which the listener recognizes as it recurs, calls up pleasure, because it is absorbed not only by the head but also by the heart and the will. In the same way, the repetition of subject material should not be a mechanical repetition by rote. Feelings stimulated by the first listening must resound again. Then pupils assimilate the material not only with their heads, but with their whole being.

Thus the connection of repetition in consciousness and with breathing is established. Both are linked to repetition in musical practice, which becomes ever more important for the child.

With small children, musical practice is not yet necessary for they imitate spontaneously. Everything is play for them. Now practice – but a *playing* (not playful!) practice – should begin. Change and breathing are its inherent and fundamental qualities. The repetition of short melodies in singing and in instrumental playing makes learning possible. Yet these must not be open-ended and unfinished. Only the balanced musical phrase (which, musically speaking, combines in and out breathing), lends itself to repeated use. You can quickly bring a class of ten-year-olds into disorder if you start musical phrases arbitrarily or interrupt and recommence them without regard to an organic rest, that is, one corresponding to the nature of the piece. The right amount of repetition brings the breathing of the child into the same harmonizing rhythm which also pervades well-chosen songs. At the same time the child is able to penetrate more deeply and fundamentally into the details of a piece. *Wakeful consciousness* is appealed to, without its becoming overtaxed. The random practice of a melody chopped up into sections is hard enough even for an adult; for a child it is almost impossible unless he were forced into doing it purely mechanically. The intellect would have to be too strongly involved, instead of practising itself becoming an art. Thus in artistic practice the opposite poles of breathing and consciousness find their balance.

4) Development

Puberty presents new tasks for the educator — which are not of their nature the easiest ones either. The growing passivity and reticence of pupils at that stage can cause great difficulties for the teacher. In music lessons, this is often more distressing for him than the broken voices of the boys, which, incidentally, in a large class should not become an excuse for giving up singing altogether. As I had to teach a lot in the middle school, I tried to find ways of overcoming this lethargy. Repetition was a great help. Yet here its limited uses had to be safeguarded. A small child is always happy to sing the same song again. Not so the fourteen-year-old. Even a single repeat can already cause grousing and complaints: Why always the same? The musician, who is used to constant repetition until he has mastered a difficulty, must restrain himself here more than usual. Why is repetitive practice so hard for the fourteen-year-old? He no longer has the natural formative force to give himself over into the breathing of a melody. His awkward bearing is an expression of this.

Should the teacher now give in and dispense with practice? No! By all means he can employ repetition, but it must be used so that it blossoms into development. Outwardly it might appear the same; inwardly it must bring enhancement, otherwise it relapses into indolence and ends up in deep gloom or resignation. And how easily and how often does such a class slip away from the teacher's control!

The teacher will now no longer repeat nicely rounded-off phrases. To start with he will intervene during the first, usually dull beginning, interrupting the complete phrase; make them sing it again, and again a third time. After this he must let the reins go, and then — if he is successful — forces proceeding from the gradually awakening personality of the young people are expressed in the song: then singing acquires the fire, still missing in the younger classes, and allows the pupils to grasp the forming-forces of music from within.

The meaning of the threefold beginning, discussed in the Beethoven example above, became clear to me in this form of practice. We saw how Beethoven checked development and through this intensified its power immensely. Such holding back awakens activity in the pupils. Where their initial attitude is perhaps still critical, with the second attempt their feeling is stimulated as positive pleasure, or negative annoyance. Pressing on with the third repeat achieves a closer connection with the passage and leads to action. I would like to call it 'putting your back into it', which proceeds, full of strength, from the experience of the self — no matter whether the driving force of the second stage was pleasure or annoyance. Experiences of this power of musical expression are important for the overcoming of puberty. We see here the identifying of phenomena which is summed up in the word 'development'.

The three stages are therefore a progression through the three soul-forces of thinking, feeling and doing. On the surface, repetition appears the same. Inwardly, the human being becomes connected ever more strongly with the passage. This law works at all differing levels. The sportsman, too, begins three times before he proceeds into action (for instance, in putting the shot, or in the threefold formula 'on your marks ...', etc.). In life it is often said: you may start three times. If you don't succeed by the third time, you won't succeed at all. In fairy-tales (which may be regarded as an artistic image of the soul-forces in play) we repeatedly find the threefold formula.

As a higher sign for this threefold appeal to the human soul, let us mention at this point the double repetition of certain rites in the rituals of different religions.

The other side of music teaching, that of the appreciation of music, poses similar problems for us in the middle school. Most pupils at this age allow a piece of music played for them to pass by without making any effort at a deeper penetration and understanding of it. The music teacher has the feeling that he is playing to a cold audience. This lack of participation manifests in pupils' restlessness, which the teacher notices with his artistic sensitivity, even if it is hardly apparent on the surface. I accustomed myself to ignore it at my first attempt, but then I stopped in the middle of a piece and after a short pause began it a second time, and, if need be, interrupted it yet a second time. Then a very quiet and brief comment was usually enough to wake the last sleeper and silence the chatter-box, and then, during the third attempt, you could feel a warm participation, something not often achieved even by adults. Here I should like to recall the repeat in Mozart which awakened consciousness, and also Riemann's demand for the training of active listening. If this form of repetition is successful in awakening the fourteen-year-olds to activity, then a foundation is laid for an understanding of the great master who used it to such perfection — namely Beethoven.

5) Transformation

Only after the young person has reached maturity can the teacher take advantage of the forces of personality which at first appear spontaneously and chaotically. These forces, however, give the possibility of grasping and understanding not only in doing and listening. Out of them the ability to reform things anew and reassess them is gradually developed from within. We stand at the stage where repetition turns into variation, or to transformation. In the musical section, I mentioned variation for the first time with the little dance from the sixteenth century (Example 39). Yet at that time variation was only superficial − in musical terminology it was only figuration. With Beethoven and Mozart it begins to penetrate into the character of the theme. A prerequisite for this is a strong personality, which can transform itself without thereby losing itself. Repetition is concentrated into a germ of what is happening.

In Romanticism, transformation comes still more often to the fore. Think of the example from Bruckner's *Fourth Symphony* (Example 78): a common note is placed within completely new, distant harmonic relationships.

Let us proceed to practical application. Students in the upper school must become capable of viewing the same thing from different angles in all fields. The teacher can illuminate a subject in a completely different way when it is repeated in lessons. In terms of musical activity this means *practising artistically*. A work first becomes filled with content when it is tackled from the most varied aspects. While practising, not only do you change from loud to soft, slow to quick in order to achieve a deeper interpretation. In the upper school you can also try with suitable pieces to alter their character, in order to find out more clearly what is unique about them. In discussing musical history you can make the attempt to fit a melody to different epochs of style by varying the accompaniment and the expression.

Here, once again, we stand at the threshold of modern times: repetition becomes transformation, metamorphosis. If the feeling for what remains constant was established in the previous years, through the practice of repetition, then it is also possible for the pupils to understand the powerful transformations which often appear in modern works.

6) The Camlness and Strength in Rhythmical Repetition in Life and in Education

'Rhythm replaces force,' says an old saying. Here rhythm is to be understood as regular repetition. The truth of this saying is confirmed everywhere. In the introduction to a collection of new songs, Caroline von Heydebrand writes:

> Rhythm belongs to the most hidden, yet strongest forces which a person needs for development. The rhythmical course of the year with its months, weeks and days, which allows an everlasting recurrence and renewal, forms the foundation of all life ... The growing individual requires rhythmical repetition for the well-being of body and soul. It is one of the most essential principles of education to structure the life and work of a child according to strict rhythms. We must never underestimate the healthy and ethical significance of rhythm in daily life.

These words, based on Caroline von Heydebrand's long educational experience, point to the important value of repetition in general education. The rhythms of time become a help for both ethical and physical health. The educator must take pains to observe them everywhere. Also, in the whole structure of lessons, it does the child good when regular order reigns. The child receives something from its schooling which will be an important support for later life. Inner calmness and inner strength can develop from this rhythmical repetition - which perhaps later can only be consistently pursued in a few aspects when we consider everything which tends to destroy rhythm today.

With this, however, we have returned to what we recognized in Bach: the eternal flux above a peaceful, divine foundation of eternal sameness. Let the words of Goethe be quoted here once more, which express our thoughts on repetition in such a perfect way:

Wenn im Unendlichen dasselbe
Sich widerholend ewig fliesst,
Das tausendfältige Gewölbe
Sich kräftig ineinander schliesst;
Strömt Lebenslust aus allen Dingen,
Dem kleinsten wie dem grössten Stern,
Und alles Drängen, alles Ringen
Ist ewig Ruh' in Gott dem Herrn.

When in the infinite the same pattern
Repeats itself in eternal flux,
And the thousandfold vault of heaven
Mutually supports itself,
Then joy of life streams from all things,
From the smallest to the greatest of stars,
And all yearning, all struggle,
Is eternal rest in God the Lord.

BIBLIOGRAPHY

ADLER, Guido. *Handbuch der Musikgeschichte I. Teil.* Heinrich Keller Verlag. Berlin. 1930

AMBROS, August Wilhelm. *Geschichte der Musik II.* Verlag von F.E.C. Leuckart. Leipzig. 1891

HERDER, J. Gottfried. *Vom Geist der Ebräischen Poesie.* Verlag Gotha. 1890

HEYDEBRAND, Caroline V. Forword to *Feierlieder des Jahres* by A. Künstler (Duplicated MS)

KURTH, Ernst. *Bruckner.* Max Hesses Verlag. 1925

LANG, Paul Henry. *Die Musik im Abendland.* Manu Verlag. Augsburg. 1947

MERSMANN, Hans. *Angewandte Musikästhetik.* Max Hesses Verlag. 1926

MERSMANN, Hans. *Musikhören.* Hans F. Menck Verlag. Frankfurt am Main. 1952

MOSER Hans-Joachim. *Lehrbuch der Musikgeschichte.* Max Hesses Verlag. 1937

PESTALOZZI, Heinrich. *Gesammelte Werke Bd. 10 Schwanengesang.* Rascher Verlag. Zürich

RIEMANN, Hugo. *Musik-Ästhetik.* Max Hesse Verlag. Leipzig. 1911

RIEMANN, Hugo. *Musiklexikon* (revised Einstein). Rascher Verlag. 1922

SCHUBERT, Friedrich. *Sophokles Oidipus Tyrannos.* Gustav Freytag Verlag. Leipzig. 1907

VALENTIN, Erich. *Wege zu Mozart.* Gustav Bosse Verlag. Regensburg. 1941